The Activating Concern

Churches and Social Welfare
Vol. I

The Activating Concern
Historical and Theological Bases

Edited By
E. Theodore Bachmann
with an
Introduction by Roswell P. Barnes

**NATIONAL COUNCIL OF THE CHURCHES
OF CHRIST IN THE U.S.A.**

CONTENTS

Once you were no people
but now you are God's people;
once you had not received mercy
but now you have received mercy.

1 Peter 2:10

INTRODUCTION

One evidence of the vitality of the churches today is their careful, honest self-examination. It arises out of strength and confidence, not out of frustration or out of uneasiness about the future.

Included in this self-examination is a restatement of basic purposes and objectives in terms clearly relevant to the present situation and persuasive to this generation. It calls for a fresh analysis of the role of the church in society, especially in relation to the many new secular institutions and the expanding operations of tax-supported agencies—federal, state, and local. This leads to a reconsideration of the churches' programs. Which programs are essential? Which contribute to the basic objectives of the churches?

This volume is one contribution to the examination of the activities of the churches in the field of social welfare, including social service, social education and action, and social research. It is concerned primarily with basic questions of principle and policy. Is social welfare a marginal and optional field in the life of the churches? Is a church under any biblical or theological mandate to work in this field, or is it impelled only by a fading tradition? Should the churches abandon the field to nonsectarian agencies and concentrate their energies and resources on what is generally described as their unique spiritual functions? If they should not abandon the field entirely, should they limit themselves to caring for their own constituents or for their own professional servants? What consideration should be given to the fact that our Roman Catholic and Jewish friends maintain very extensive programs and institutions providing welfare services?

Some denominations have numerous welfare institutions and agencies; others have very few. There are wide variations of policy and practice. Perhaps the variations are more in practice, arising from history and tradition, rather than from consciously defined policy.

Such questions and considerations have given rise to a sense of need for counseling together, for sharing convictions and traditions, so that each denomination may have the benefit of wide and thoughtful consultation as it seeks to define its basic objectives grounded on biblical, theological, and historical justification. Such a sharing of insights is necessary for sound planning by the churches with regard to their co-operative activities in the whole field of social welfare, whether in the local community or in overseas relief and reconstruction.

We know of no one who desires or expects to develop one theological definition of the grounds for Christian social welfare. We

1

believe in the creativity of freedom and the stimulation of diversity. There is, however, a widespread desire in many of the churches to make more careful statements of their reasons for, and purposes in, their social welfare activities. It is assumed that certain purposes will be generally shared by the churches and that they can be stated as the grounds for co-operative enterprises.

The churches are more alike in their practices in social welfare than in their reasons for them, and more alike in their reasons than in their explanations of them. An outsider, hearing us talk, would be dismayed by our differences; seeing us act, he would be convinced that we are in general agreement. Herein lies one of the interesting and significant aspects of interdenominational co-operation. Participation in common practices demonstrates a practical Christian unity and facilitates co-operation in examining the basic principles and presuppositions which are largely shared among us.

The relation of social welfare to other functions of the churches needs careful consideration. It should not, and cannot appropriately, be segregated and isolated. Much of the social welfare work of the churches was begun and is continued because it was considered to be essential to the missionary and evangelistic work. It certainly did not arise from a sub-Christian ethical humanitarianism. It should not be justified now merely in terms of abstract or academic sociological and economic analysis of society.

Our organizational patterns have unfortunately contributed to the segregation of social welfare from other functions of the churches. Administrative necessity or expediency that puts various functions into units of organization—sometimes competing for attention and support—gives a false impression of separateness of function. This is conducive to fragmentation and to rivalry for priority listing in a scale of urgency or essentiality.

Necessary professional specialization also contributes to distortion of perspective and isolation. Social welfare, evangelism, education, missions are all interrelated and interdependent. One turns to the twelfth chapter of 1 Corinthians and sees a new relevance in the exposition of the diversities of gifts and the different members of the one body. Social welfare is an essential member of the body of the church, but only one of several interdependent members.

This volume is really a background document for use in preparation for the National Conference on the Churches and Social Welfare, to be held at Cleveland, Ohio, in November, 1955. It is a "homework" assignment to be read, not only by participants in the Conference, but by all who are interested in the development of clearer policies in our churches. It will not be out of date after the Cleveland Conference. It is more revealing of the churches and their various insights than of their social welfare programs. The activities of the churches are more fully reported in a companion volume. Yet, here we may gain understanding of the various approaches to definitions of the role of the church in society. Such understanding is a prerequisite to constructive participation in any ecumenical intercourse.

The reader should be cautioned against expecting that the pattern of the Cleveland Conference will reflect the emphases of this volume. These papers are concerned primarily with the basic policies underlying the corporate activities of national denominations. Those policies may or may not be discernibly reflected in the work of the local congregations of the respective denominations. The major portion of the service of the local church is to its own constituents and its own community. The sum total of the social welfare work of all the local churches is vastly more significant in terms of the bulk of service rendered and the impact upon society than the work of the national organizations of those churches. It is hoped that the Cleveland Conference will consider the comprehensive whole, including national and local. The mandates and motivations underlying the total enterprise are analyzed here, but the illustrations are predominantly national.

It would be a mistake to assume that every minister or member of a local church will feel that the statement in this volume describing his denomination describes him. There are wide variations within most of the denominations. Local situations differ according to the nature of the community. A member of the Reformed Church in America may be in agreement with the analysis of the theological positions of his church and at the same time feel that the statement about the Society of Friends appeals to him in terms of motivation to action. Or a Congregationalist might accept both the statement about his own denomination and the principles of the Episcopalian statement. It is quite likely that some readers—we hope many—will upon finishing the volume say, with new understanding and gratitude, "I believe in the Holy Catholic Church." At the same time, he will have increased appreciation of the contribution of his own communion.

A further word is needed with regard to the genesis and nature of this book. The planning committee for the Cleveland Conference requested churches representing the various traditions to prepare statements in three parts, dealing with matters of authority, function, and comity in Christian welfare work. A guide for the preparation of these statements was drawn up by the editor of this volume and is set forth in full in the first chapter. The writers of the statements, however, were granted considerable freedom of development.

The resulting statements are unofficial yet responsible. Several denominations set up commissions to prepare them; others desig-

3

nated authors. No writer was selected either by the committee or by the editor.

The editor, E. Theodore Bachmann, is well qualified by training, experience, and general competence. He is professor of church history and missions and director of graduate studies at the Pacific Lutheran Theological Seminary at Berkeley, California. He was formerly professor of church history (1942-1948) at Chicago Lutheran Seminary. Earlier he had served congregations in Pottsville, Pennsylvania, and in Wilmington, Delaware.

Dr. Bachmann has degrees from Haverford College; Lutheran Theological Seminary at Philadelphia; Harvard; and the University of Chicago. He has also studied in Europe and the Near East.

His acquaintance with welfare is even broader than his academic and pastoral experience. His father was for many years head of the Lutheran deaconess work in Philadelphia. Dr. Bachmann was also for two and one-half years deputy chief of the Religious Affairs Branch, first in the U. S. Military Government in Germany and then in the Office of the U. S. High Commissioner.

ROSWELL P. BARNES

INVENTORY OF
CHRISTIAN SOCIAL CONCERN

A visiting theologian from Europe, upon closer acquaintance with the American scene, observed a contrast between the situation as he knew it at home and as he found it here. "We in Europe," declared Hans Asmussen, "have laid great emphasis on theological knowledge, yet as Christians we have known better than we have done. But I think you Americans, with your so-called activism in church life, have done better than you know."

This observation provides a clue to the purpose of a study initiated by the National Council of Churches for a deeper and theologically more aware understanding of what the communions within its membership have been doing in the field of social welfare. While the Christian faith responds to God in worship, it expresses itself in service to fellow men. As worship and service belong together, they grow at their deepest out of a redemptive, Christocentric theology that recognizes the interdependence of individuals within society and the dependence of all upon God. That such recognition has been but partially matched by achievement is one of the stubborn and tragic facts of Christian history. But that the outreach and the concern continues, and manifests itself in countless ways, reveals something of the life-giving Spirit of God among the churches in our uneasy day.

To appraise the theological basis and functional development of social concern among the member bodies in the National Council of the Churches of Christ in the U.S.A., a statement was requested from each. In order that the thinking in such diverse bodies might be stimulated along given lines, and comparable statements be produced, a *guide* was prepared. This guide, loaded with questions, was divided into three parts. The first sought to ascertain the basis of *authority* for Christian social concern in each communion; the second called for a description of that church's *function* in the area of social welfare; while the third asked for a description of *comity* with other churches or agencies active in the same area. The questions, while comprehensive, endeavored also to provide opportunity for self-examination on the part of the several church bodies. Those who did the writing know that theirs was an often difficult and sometimes impossible task, with things being requested on which data were not always available.

In order that the statements as presented in the following chapters may be better understood and appreciated, the guide to their preparation is here reproduced in full.

Authority

The basis of Christian welfare work. In the light of the theological and historical position and growth of your church body, what is the place of biblical authority in the development of a sense of responsibility in the field of social welfare? Is such biblical authority considered basic? Does it share its place with humanitarian or other authority? In terms of Christian ethics, what is it that gives the Christian in your church the right to speak and act with conviction in relation to human need and social problems? What is it that gives the churches and the communion the right or responsibility to speak and act in response to social needs? How have these ethical concepts of your communion been affected by changing theological emphases, such as neo-orthodoxy, the social gospel and earlier movements?

The motivation for Christian welfare work. What has been the apparent motivation for rendering Christian service in the field of welfare on the part of the people in your communion? What kind of biblical, theological, cultural, social, or humanitarian emphases have been distinctive in the preaching, teaching, or missioning of your church, and how may these have played a part in motivating welfare work? To what extent have influences played a part which emanated from other churches or from movements outside the churches, either in this country or abroad? What has been the role of justice versus love in moving the conscience of people to initiate and support social education, social action, and/or social research? Has there been a strong pull to care "for our own," or has the stronger appeal come from underprivileged and disadvantaged economic, ethnic or racial out-groups? To what extent has motivation been influenced by changing social and economic conditions, e.g. immigration, war, financial depression, urbanization, secularization, etc.?

Function

Social service. [Social service is here understood to mean mainly remedial work using established procedures with individuals and relatively small groups as done by church-related welfare agencies, or by nonsectarian agencies owing their initial impulse to the activity of members of your church. Increasingly there are also preventive aspects of social service, reflecting in part the recent emphases on mental health and preventive medicine.]

What do you regard as your communion's distinctive approach to social service? What are the areas of need in which your church has been most active? What influenced your people to enter these areas? Since historical perspectives are important, when did you enter upon each major area and with what purposes or objectives? Have these objectives changed, and if so, why?

6

What policy have you followed in social service: to initiate and then turn over to others? Or, to initiate, relate to the church as a continuing function, modifying programs and services as changing conditions required? Or some other policy? Why has the communion followed this policy? Has there been any noticeable change in policy? When and why?

Many church bodies have agencies operative in the following areas: family service; maternity and child care; hospitals, sanatoria, and convalescent homes; chaplaincy services; group work agencies; camps and vacation services; hospices and residence clubs and shelters; specialized services (to seamen, migrants, displaced persons, etc.); homes for the aged and infirm.

Social action. [Although it is difficult to make sharp distinctions among the terms social service, social action and social education, social action is here understood to mean the churches' direct efforts to achieve social reform, social justice, and the like.

While church-related programs of social service (III) are mainly concerned with rendering direct aid through established procedures to individuals and relatively small groups striving to meet their own physical, mental and social needs, social action is mainly concerned with improving social conditions which are related to the welfare of the social order. Its form of expression is generally less through social service agencies and more through specific groups, societies, boards of other church-related organizational forms. The method of action, moreover, is understood as varying from officially adopted resolutions to publicity promoted agitation that achieves the desired changes at local, regional, or national levels; either voluntarily or by legislation or other forms of legal enforcement.]

The range of your church's share in social action, when seen in historical as well as current perspective, would include examples from a variety of fields. Here are some: the abolition of slavery, temperance, women's rights, the condition of labor, industrial relations, public education, housing, the causes of delinquency and crime, the treatment of offenders, the proper utilization of mass media (e.g. comics, press, radio, TV, films), corruption in politics, unfair practices in business and economic life, military training, international relations, war and atomic weapons, the utilization of leisure, the problems of refugees, migrants, displaced persons; special problems of rural as well as urban society, etc.

Does your communion have a distinctive approach to social action? In what areas has it been most vocal and active? What major influences led to the selection of these areas? When? With what purposes and objectives? Through what agencies of the communion?

What significant changes have taken place with regard to your communion's approach to social action? What influences seem to have been involved in these changes? What are the present trends?

Social education. [Social education is here understood as the process whereby the membership in your church body is sensitized and made responsive to such needs and problems in society as warrant or demand the concern of Christians. Social education is therefore intimately related to social service (III) and to social action (IV).]

As a process social education is multiform and diffuse, but examples from your church body should be available from a wide variety of sources. Among such sources is the place of biblical teaching and theology as geared to man's concern for his fellow man, and for the shouldering of Christian responsibility in society as part of man's accountability to God. Related to such teaching and theology is the array of modern knowledge about man and society; a knowledge drawn from a variety of fields and professions.

How does such an informed concern find expression in your church? In preaching? In Sunday school? In study and discussion groups? In released-time and other weekday religious instruction? In confirmation or membership classes? In lecture forums? In the national, regional, and local programming of church activities? In church-sponsored publications? In officially adopted statements commended for study? In the preparation of study materials for church schools? For young people's and adult groups? In the publication policies of church boards, and through incentives offered by them in this field? In the curricula of church-related colleges? In church-sponsored programs among students and faculty on non-church campuses? In theological seminaries? In schools training church workers? In interprofessional orientation and discussions? What has your church body been doing to develop a Christian concept of vocation among its members; thus relating the Christian faith to the day's work and to a sense of informed social duty? Has your communion always been concerned in America about social education? Have there been noticeable changes in concern, in objectives? in methods? in results? What were the major influences? What are the present trends?

Social research. [Social research is here understood as a process whereby demonstrable or tested information related to the social concern of the churches is systematically gathered, analyzed, synthesized, and interpreted by scientific procedures. It involves more than taking a census of agencies and institutions, listing their addresses and assets. Some communions may never have engaged in

8

social research; some may have done so in consultation or partnership with specialized nonchurch agencies. At times a program of social research may have been financially aided by foundations or other outside sources. Social research is relevant to many problems in society with which Christians should be concerned and often serves as a basis for programs of social education (V), as well as social action (IV) and social service (III).]

How long has your church body been gathering facts or developing techniques in the field of social research? With what objectives? With what results? What has been the role of special committees, commissions, or working parties? Of full-time or part-time personnel, specially trained and working in conjunction with what national, regional or local agencies of the church? What encouragement has been given for graduate work in social research? To what extent have graduate students in social work or in other professional centers been guided to do social research in specific areas of need? What use has been made of theological seminaries to promote or engage in social research? What other agencies have shared in this task, and how have they done it?

What has been done to single out, investigate and study intensively such problems as come under social action (IV) or social service (III)? What have been the subjects of most concern in your program of social research?

Sometimes related to the general field of inquiry, although rarely if ever to the process properly known as social research, are interprofessional and interoccupational meetings oriented to study specific areas of common concern. What kinds of interprofessional and interoccupational fellowships or partnerships has your communion encouraged for this purpose? For example: pastors and psychiatrists; pastors and physicians; pastors and social workers; pastors and labor leaders; and many other combinations—including also Christian laymen meeting with non-Christians in specific fields of inquiry?

Comity

Co-operation with other churches. The field of social welfare is conducive to co-operation among churches. How and when did this get underway in your church body? In what areas of interest? With which churches? How is it continuing today? What types of projects have been most effective when undertaken jointly? What has been the effect of co-operation upon the response or responsiveness of your own membership?

What have been the roles of city and state councils of churches, of the National Council of Churches and its predecessor agencies in promoting or implementing such co-operation from the standpoint of your communion?

9

What co-operative situations has your communion experienced in relation to Roman Catholic or Jewish agencies, if any?

Co-operation with nonsectarian agencies, voluntary and public. A point of departure might be the nonsectarian agencies which owe their origin to the interest of members of your churches. (See above, III.) What kind of co-operative situations has your communion experienced in relation to nonsectarian voluntary agencies? In relation to public agencies? How has such co-operation proved fruitful in referrals and supplementary services? In the making of policy? In social planning? In common action for specific legislation? In responding to regional or nationwide social needs? In international welfare work (CRALOG, CROP, etc.)? What, if any, have been the relations of your communion (officially or informally) with schools of social work? To what extent may or should church and state co-operate in meeting the welfare needs of a free society?

THE CHURCH OF THE BRETHREN

2

A struggle for religious freedom marked the rise of the Brethren. Shortly after their origin in Germany, as conservative Dunkers, most of the group after 1719 came to Pennsylvania. From there they eventually spread to other parts of the country. Known for their opposition to class distinction and to war, their temperate and simple life reflects a practical application of New Testament ways. Their membership of some 200,000, with headquarters in Elgin, Illinois, has become widely known through the activities of the Brethren Service Commission. Since 1945 this Commission has rendered extensive relief services overseas. Under its direction, also, the following statement has been prepared, with Desmond W. Bittinger, chairman; Jefferson H. Mathis, J. Aldene Ecker, and W. Harold Row, secretary.

The Basis of Christian Welfare Work

Christian social concern in the Church of the Brethren dates from the time of its founding in western Germany in 1708. In their almost total migration to Eastern Pennsylvania by 1729, their subsequent movements southward to Virginia, westward to Kansas and on to the Pacific Coast, the Brethren have evidenced a practical concern for the poor and the distressed. Alexander Mack, the principal founder, sacrificed all of his considerable property in an effort to help his fellow Brethren who were persecuted especially for their convictions on peace. Settling first in Germantown, near Philadelphia, the early Brethren maintained their "poor box." Later they were publicly commended for heroic service during a yellow fever epidemic in Philadelphia.

Until World War I, the Church of the Brethren confined most of its social service activities to its immediate communities. Response to human suffering was spontaneous when the need was close at hand, but limited when the need was distant.

Theologically, the Church of the Brethren has been biblically centered and essentially nonsystematic. It has never formulated a creed but has claimed the New Testament as its rule of faith. The Brethren have been for the most part moderate literalists in biblical interpretation. Imitation of Jesus has been a constant theme. Favorite Scriptures have been the Sermon on the Mount, the healing miracles, the exhortations to compassion, meekness, and nonviolence. Until influenced to some extent by the fundamentalism and the "spiritual" emphasis of the present century, the Brethren never ques-

11

tioned the essential religious duty to render immediate service to those in need as an expression of Christian love. Today, Christian social service is considered one of the three great works of the church.

The Motivation for Christian Welfare Work

There have been two sources of the Christian social concern of the Brethren. The first has been *the natural sympathy of the human heart*. Though this is generally considered to be the basis of naturalistic ethics, i.e., rooted in human nature, it is also one of the bases of Christian social service. Brethren have lived close to the soil and in intimate personal relationships with their neighbors, so this natural sympathy of the human heart has been given rather free reign to express itself in social service. Even today when our program has become more complex and often is less immediately personal, this appeal continues to be effective among our constituency.

The second source of the Christian social concern of the Brethren has been *the Judeo-Christian tradition of love of God and love of man*. This provides the basis for a theistic or biblical ethics, grounded in the nature and activity of God. Brethren have understood God primarily in terms of love. They have conceived discipleship as love of God and love for man. The Brethren have regarded the two great commandments as equally binding. The first commandment issues in worship and dedication, the second in unselfish service to one's fellow men. This service, however, is understood not in the modern sense of "charity," showing "love" to our neighbor in order to please God, but rather in terms of the New Testament Greek word *agape*, serving our neighbor because of God's love for us and in us. This has resulted for the most part in a program of helping people to help themselves. One of our number has called this, "charity with self-respect." Related to this is our practice of encouraging the recipient of material aid to pass on the gift to another in need.

These two sources of Christian social concern—natural sympathy of the human heart and the Judeo-Christian concept of love of God and love of Man—have produced a reservoir of goodwill which has evidenced itself occasionally in comparatively large scale programs of social welfare, especially in the fields of relief and rehabilitation. Noteworthy among these have been the Heifer Project, the relief goods processing centers, and the refugee resettlement program.

Brethren gradually have come to the conviction that goodwill projects are not enough. Knowledge, particularly that from the social sciences, must be added to make goodwill *effective*. This leads beyond social service which is ameliorative to social action which is remedial. This intentional development in the Church of the Brethren has emerged only within the past quarter century and more especially since World War II. Besides, the welfare work of the

12

Brethren has been stimulated and enhanced by its position on war and peace. Since its founding, the Church of the Brethren has been pacifist in doctrine and fairly consistently so in practice.

The Brethren have been caught up in most of the social movements which have swept America. However, because they were, until recently, largely rural and fairly secure in Brethren communities, they were seldom found in the role of reformers. Economically, the Brethren clustered around the typically Protestant lower middle class. Politically, they were in general a little to the right of center. Until the last two decades it was a rare exception to find Brethren in the leadership of labor unions, political parties, social clubs, or even interchurch movements. Today active attention is given by more and more Brethren to labor-management relationships, political action, city planning, and interchurch and interfaith activities in their local communities.

The Brethren have tended to emphasize love and to minimize justice in their Christian social concerns. This resulted from (1) the central conviction of the Brethren about the nature of God as love, and the discipleship requirement of obedience to the Son of God who "went about doing good," and (2) the lack of sufficient understanding of the dynamics of political, economic, and social structures. While *love* has been a constantly used term in Brethren preaching and teaching, the concepts of *justice* and *power* have been seldom used. Yet there is a growing concern among Brethren that an ethic relating love to power and to justice, as well as each to the other, is an imperative duty. Brethren have just begun to face squarely the neo-orthodox charges of "irresponsibility" and "irrelevancy" as applied to Christian pacifism as a social action philosophy. However, the Brethren will probably continue to give first priority and allegiance to the God of love, even as they recognize him more fully as the God also of justice.

One of the clearest principles of Brethren social welfare today is that service is to be rendered to the most needy without regard to race, creed, or nationality. In earlier days when social welfare was limited mostly to mutual aid among those in the immediate community, preference for those holding membership in the denomination was probably the rule—though this is by no means conclusively so. When, however, the Brethren went beyond their own communities, and especially when social service programs were established abroad, it became a consistent principle that service was to be given to the *neediest and most neglected*, without prejudice as to his ethic origin or religious affiliation.

A second principle of Brethren social welfare practice is that whenever possible the service rendered is to be related to a local church. This generally means a non-Brethren church or occasionally a non-Protestant church, since most service is carried on in communities where there is no Brethren church. Such church-related-ness is stressed both as a principle and as a strategy. Since this service is church-related, it should strengthen the church universal wherever it serves. A local church, moreover, provides a well established social structure with which to relate immediate as well as long term social service. In some instances, however, the service is necessarily related to nonchurch institutions.

In short, Brethren believe that every human need has spiritual significance, and must be met on its own level. Brethren have, therefore, placed strong emphasis upon material aid. "For I was hungry and you gave me food . . . I was naked and you clothed me. . . . " So, without neglecting evangelism and nurture, the church seeks to fulfill one of its basic tasks when it gives food to the hungry, recognizing that social service in a ravaged world is a valid ministry of the Church of Christ.

Social Service

Social service, among the Brethren, grows out of their close sympathy to human need. Historically, Brethren social service has largely been direct charity. As early as 1770 a local congregation had established and regularly financed a home for a widow and her children. Soon homes for the aged started at various locations throughout the brotherhood. Some were very small, inadequately financed or supervised. Approximately sixteen homes continued through the years, with thirteen operating at the present time. All of these are under the control of district trustee boards, with the Brethren Service Commission providing an advisory service. The majority of these homes now function in close co-operation with state welfare agencies.

Children's homes and orphanages were established soon after the homes for the aged. These were a little more closely related to the national boards of the church. Gradually Brethren orphanages became receiving homes or adoption agencies, and several closed entirely. Today no Brethren orphanage operates as a permanent residence for children.

A total of six Brethren hospitals are operated in Puerto Rico, Africa, and India. The only Brethren hospital in the United States was established in 1920 in Chicago as Bethany Hospital and continues to be related to the denomination through a trustee board named by a free association of individual sponsors. Bethany Hospital is financed by its own services and by general solicitation from the Church of the Brethren constituency.

The most distinctive social service of the Church of the Brethren has been in the area of relief and rehabilitation. This activity outside of America began in 1895 with Brethren providing material aid to the famine sufferers in India in the area of their mission work. In

1908 a similar service was rendered in China. Brethren first sent material aid, money, and personnel to areas where no mission of theirs was established, or contemplated, when they supported the Near East Foundation in feeding starving Armenians in 1918-1922. Again in the Spanish Civil War, help was given in co-operation with the Friends and Mennonites. The same was done in 1938-1942 for the Chinese refugees from the Sino-Japanese War. When the need arose to provide alternative service for conscientious objectors to military service, this was done in co-operation with the Friends, Mennonites, and other communions by working out agreements with the Selective Service system.

These varied activities led in 1941 to the formation of the Brethren Service Commission. Since that time, this Commission has represented the Brethren in areas of social education, social action, and social service. Through it they have carried on extensive relief and rehabilitation activities in many countries. Material aid centers at New Windsor, Maryland; Nappanee, Indiana; and Modesto, California; and a system of trucking depots and collection centers across the country have supported these operations.

Brethren have initiated services in areas of need and then have offered them to some existing agency or have joined in the formation of a new agency. Conspicuous examples of this pattern have been the Heifer Project which became an interfaith agency in 1952; the Interchurch Service to Greek Villages which was spearheaded by the Brethren but which is now administered by an interchurch committee under the World Council of Churches, and the teen-age Student Exchange program which is now in the process of becoming interchurch.

Social Action, Education, and Research

Social action and social service are mutually inclusive in much of the welfare work of the Brethren. Interest in social action has increased sharply within recent decades. Peace education has been the most prominent concern. In World War II this was coupled with opposition to the military draft, and implemented with the setting up of work camps for conscientious objectors. In 1944 and again in 1952 Brethren concentrated on opposing legislation for Universal Military Training.

Balancing such negation has been the positive development of the Brethren Volunteer Service, and the Brethren Alternative Service. Since 1948, the B.V.S. has enlisted some 700 young people for service of one to three years in the U.S.A. or overseas. Trained at New Windsor, Maryland, they have gone out on a dozen different types of projects, such as migrant camps, foreign relief, and the like. Meanwhile, the Alternative Service program has co-operated with Selective Service in receiving not only Brethren but others for the regular two-year assignment to units in mental hospitals and elsewhere.

Brethren are devoting increased effort to such social education and research as will best undergird their service and action. They seek to relate the principles of Christian ethics to major social issues, particularly as these come into focus in Washington or other political centers. Similarly ecumenical concerns are brought home to the constituency. Means to these ends include conferences, workshops, campus institutes, seminars at the United Nations and in Washington.

The latter have drawn as many as 300 young people at one time, and have stimulated keen interest in political issues and legislative processes. Paralleling these measures have been specially drafted statements on war (1948), race relations (1950), and economic life (1951).

Close contact has been maintained with teachers of sociology and religion in the six Brethren colleges, with Bethany Seminary, and with students doing graduate work in the social sciences. Permanent committees, utilizing personnel of this type, along with experts in these fields, have been set up to advise the Brethren Service Commission.

Research has consisted mainly in questionnaires on specific matters. The findings of non-Brethren agencies have often provided helpful data for guidance and planning.

❁   ❁   ❁

Co-operation with Other Churches

For the past decades Brethren have co-operated with other churches in welfare programs. Their closest ties have been with the two other communions which have a historic peace testimony, the Mennonites and the Friends. They were partners in the Civilian Public Service program during World War II. Relief and rehabilitation projects have likewise been undertaken co-operatively. In a wider context, Brethren have co-operated extensively in the National Council of Churches, through Church World Service, and in the World Council of Churches. They have also helped to found and sustain the Church Peace Mission and the National Board of Religious Objectors.

The Service Commission has had helpful associations with both Roman Catholic and Jewish agencies. The Catholic Rural Life Association was one of the first participants in the Heifers for Relief project.

There was similar partnership in connection with the Council of Relief Agencies Licensed for Operation in Germany (CRALOG), and with other joint undertakings.

16

Co-operation with Nonsectarian Agencies, Voluntary and Public

Since 1945 there has been a strong increase in the co-operation of Brethren with governmental and voluntary agencies. In addition to activities already mentioned, Brethren were responsible for recruiting and supervising thousands of cattle attendants for UNRRA shipments to Europe. Also under UNRRA the Brethren provided a tractor team of fifty for land reclamation in China, and a rehabilitation team for Ethiopia. Other wartime and postwar co-operative services included assistance to relocated Japanese-Americans; participation in War Prisoners' Aid of the World's Y.M.C.A., in the Co-operative for American Remittances to Europe (CARE), in the Christian Rural Overseas Program (CROP), in American Relief for Korea (ARK).

Brethren have also shared in the American Point Four program for underdeveloped countries, and in United Nations agencies like the World Health Organization, the International Children's Emergency Fund. Their participation in projects like these has given Brethren an opportunity to share the spiritual motivation which they believe is essential to the ultimate success also of governmental operations. Yet Brethren believe that the church must remain true to its own mission and heritage, and never allow itself to become the tool of government or of some secular purpose.

THE CONGREGATIONAL
CHRISTIAN CHURCHES

3

Since its New England beginnings in 1620, Congregationalism has influenced religion in America. This influence, relatively greater before the twentieth century, roots in a Calvinist heritage as modified by democratic, intellectual, humanitarian, and other forces. Identification with the community has come naturally to Congregationalists, the social gospel being a fair example.

The Christian Churches, arising in the 1790's, represent a blend of Methodist, Baptist, and Presbyterian strains. Their name expressed their desire to overcome denominational divisions. Like the Congregationalists, their church life and polity were democratic.

In 1931 these two groups merged. The nearly one million and a half members of the Congregational Christian Churches are strongest in New England, in parts of the Midwest and Pacific Coast. (A merger with the Evangelical and Reformed Church is in progress.) Their social concern is described in a statement prepared by Victor Obenhaus, of the Chicago Theological Seminary faculty, in partnership with a specially appointed commission.

The Basis of Christian Welfare Work

For Congregational Christians the Bible is regarded as containing the record of God's relations with men and of the life which is possible where men live in faithfulness to God. Specific biblical injunctions are binding as they illumine the value of life lived in such faithfulness. Thus a concern for human welfare derives from the conviction that God's kingdom is served by men in accordance as they do his will. Biblical authority for welfare resides in the total import of the biblical message summarized in the command to love others because of God's love for us. Besides, humanitarianism looms large in the thinking and action of Congregational Christians but the term "humanitarianism" cannot itself be separated from its theological implications.

Lacking a binding and uniform creed there is nevertheless a common commitment presupposed in the Congregational Christian communion out of which grows an imperative for social concern and action. This lies in the covenant relationship with God and one's fellow men. It is an inescapable involvement of human beings with God and with one another. This, believe the adherents of this communion, is the continuance of the biblical heritage. From it stems the right and necessity to speak and act with conviction in matters of human concern.

Awareness that personal responsibility is insufficient re-enforces a united and co-operative effort. A sense of responsibility for the totality of society has evolved.

The Congregational Christian communion found its first full opportunity for expression on American soil. During its first two centuries authorization for community well-being sprang from the idea of the covenanted fellowship here. However, a realization that peoples in other areas of the globe were without the gospel gave rise to the first foreign missionary agency. The "darkness" in which others were living seemed to be a combination of ignorance regarding the message of salvation and low standards of living. Thus the gospel they were impelled to share was deemed to have significance for the whole gamut of life.

In company with other communions, which also stressed a broadly trained ministry, there were proliferated agencies and organizations for meeting social ills and understanding the causes giving rise to them. The social message of both the Old and the New Testaments became authoritative. Justice, it was believed, constituted an integral part of the love ethic of Jesus. Acquaintance with the Hebrew prophets and the Sermon on the Mount disposed individuals and groups to act in accordance therewith. Official emphases of the denomination undergirded efforts to develop an "action to match our gospel." This was posited on the widely held conviction that "the gospel of Jesus can be the solvent of social as well as of other problems."

The changing theological complexion of America found substantial response in this communion. Less than twenty years after an official endorsement of the sentence quoted above the same representative body approved the following statement: "God the Creator of heaven and earth has revealed himself and his will for us in Jesus Christ; because he so loved the world that he spared not his own Son, we find in the life, teaching, death and resurrection of Jesus Christ the disclosure of God's own forgiving, sacrificial, and transforming love for all mankind."

From a pioneering covenant-minded fellowship, then through establishment as *the* church in New England, there emerged a wave of passionate concern for the elevation of all life and for reducing suffering and its causes.

The Motivation for Christian Welfare

Meeting human need as a means for expressing the love of Christ is the theme which runs through official and unofficial proclamations in Congregational history. Closely allied with this theme is the desire to "Christianize society." There seems to be a recognized tie between them. A Christianized society would presumably assure justice and alleviate the misery due to injustice and exploitation of the weak.

The first large scale welfare concern in which the denomination participated was the effort to eliminate slavery. After Emancipation its concern was the welfare of the Freedmen. Back of this movement was a conviction of man's dignity as bestowed by his Creator and a desire to establish justice for a group yet unable to defend itself.

Applied first to the slavery issue and later to all other social issues, is the pronouncement appearing early in the nineteenth century "whatever does violence to public virtue and debauches the heart is to be dreaded especially when government becomes the actor." The missionary as the servant of Christ and the gospel's interpreter "must take the lead in all educational enterprises and see that the fountains of knowledge are kept pure and everywhere open to all classes and to both sexes."

On both the foreign and home fields it is apparent that motives were manifold rather than attributable to single sources. Schools and hospitals were sustained to facilitate wholesomeness of body and mind wherewith self-realization might be more fully attained. "The cup of cold water" was supplied with the assumption that the recipient will realize that it had been given "in My Name."

Example of a life lived after the manner of our Lord has been deemed both a fulfillment of the imperative and a means of extending the gospel. In circumstances where hostility to the active extension of the Christian faith has prevailed, *example* in welfare service has been relied upon heavily. Especially has this been true in areas dominated by Islamic culture, in settlement houses and among peoples of non-Protestant religious affiliation.

Running throughout the emphasis upon restoration of health and elimination of hinderances to personal fulfillment is the conviction that *to be able to take advantage of opportunity* is a prerequisite to religious wholesomeness. Availability of education then must be included in any hierarchy of welfare values. Nor is it to be presumed that the saving of souls played little or no part in Congregational Christian motivation. Yet the weight of emphasis lies more heavily in the other areas mentioned.

Significantly, it was the leadership of mission agencies of this denomination which strongly and successfully undergirded the efforts to secure an official Council for Social Action. The latter group has applied itself to the task of fostering justice as an integral and indispensable aspect of implementing the gospel of love in society. Historically, the Congregational Christian denomination has contributed substantially to the ideas and action identified with the social gospel, sometimes characterized as America's most distinctive contribution to religious life.

❖   ❖   ❖

Social Service

The distinctiveness which marks this denomination's social concern and action stems from its origins and its early experience on this continent. Instead of providing relief through permanent institutions under ecclesiastical auspices its remedial activities have had a temporary quality about them because of an implicit expectation that with adequate opportunity through education and training the causes of the personal and social maladjustment would be reduced. Where need has continued to persist such as in the areas of physical disability, religious sponsorship of continuing organizations has been justified on the ground of setting an example for other private or public agencies.

In the foreign mission program, as already indicated, it was early recognized that salvation was facilitated through helping to make the person whole. Hospitals on the mission field, both abroad and at home, emulate our Lord's concern for those who are sick and provide an example more eloquent than words conveying the way in which the Christian faith expresses itself toward all of God's children. The emphasis upon healing of body and mind contributed to the patient's understanding of the fuller meaning of the Christian gospel. An enterprise begun in 1810, has continued with this emphasis until the present day under the American Board of Commissioners for Foreign Missions.

Following the emancipation of the slaves the American Missionary Association conducted some five hundred schools throughout the South to enable those who were formerly the victims of slavery or a war impoverished area of the nation to provide for themselves more adequately. This self-help movement in education extended to the disadvantaged white population also. As public education became more widespread emphasis was given to higher education. Today a substantial number of first-rate Negro colleges attest to the validity of this movement among the descendants of slaves. Berea College in Kentucky symbolizes a similar interest among white young people.

Similar educational interest has extended to the Indian American. The denominational welfare activities have included the encouragement of education, a social work ministry, a token medical service. Perhaps most important has been the attempt to sensitize public agencies dealing with the Indian American and foster an acquaintance on the part of church people with the nature of the Indian situation in this country.

With the influx of large numbers of immigrants into the American metropolitan centers, Congregational Christians provided substantial aid for the operating of *settlement houses*. It was assumed that the example of Christian concern and a desire to help in the transi-

21

tion from Old World ways to the New would fit the newcomers to this country to become "solid Christian citizens." Significantly, the first professorship in Christian sociology at any American theological seminary was held by Professor Graham Taylor whose laboratory was a social settlement which he founded—the Chicago Commons.

Along with the rise of public agencies, attention of the denomination was directed to inequities evident in the domestic scene as the result of industrialization and of developments on the international scene. Most recent of the needs calling forth action are those resulting from World War II and the Korean War. Both direct relief and reconstruction aided by formal and informal educational activities have been given. The Congregational Christian Service Committee, closely correlated with work of other denominations through Church World Service, recently stated: "The love of Christ constrains us when we see children of the Most High hungry and naked, sick or in any kind of imprisonment. To make that love effective, ministries of compassion have been set up that enable those members of the Body of Christ who are relatively strong to bear some of the burdens of the weak."

Where possible it has been the policy of the denomination to encourage public agencies to assume welfare and educational functions. The assumption behind this practice has been (1) that the needs are not those of any particular parochial group, and (2) that sensitive Christians in the body politic will help to assure a quality of treatment such that the kinds of interest originally evidenced by the church may be continued.

Social Action

For almost two centuries the Congregational churches in New England were the established church. They were charged with the responsibility for public morality and community welfare. Though establishment ceased the concern for community welfare continued. "Community welfare" included a variety of interests. From its beginnings, for example, the temperance movement in America has been substantially influenced by Congregational leadership. Likewise the first peace societies were largely instigated by members of the same communion.

A Congregational clergyman, Theodore D. Weld, and his seventy disciples who carried the anti-slavery crusade throughout the middlewest were among the most influential of the Abolitionists. As indicated earlier, the role of the American Missionary Association, founded in 1846, looms large in the annals of efforts on behalf of opportunities for Negroes.

The social gospel, greatly influenced by the theology of Horace Bushnell, emerged around economic issues, the relationship of labor and management and the welfare of workers in an industrial society. The latter movement is synonymous with the names of Gladden, Strong, Tucker, Herron, Taylor and many other Congregationalists. A Commission on Social Service and other agencies of like title, helped to focus the denomination's attention on major social issues. Among its objectives were : 1) "to make known the social principles of Christianity; 2) to arouse the spirit of social service in our churches."

In 1925 "a statement of social ideals" was prepared and adopted by the denomination. Among other things it said, "We believe in making the social and spiritual ideals of Jesus our test for community as well as for individual life; in strengthening and deepening the interpersonal relationship of the individual with God, and recognizing his obligation and duty to society."

Between the period marking the rise of the social gospel and the events following World War I a noticeable change of climate appeared. The too sanguine expectations that economic and international tensions would yield to greater awareness of "the principles of Jesus" had declined. Those responsible for interpreting the relevance of the Christian faith to social issues had kept pace with and helped further a profounder theological understanding of the social issues and the world situation. The concern with these issues has not abated even though the appraisal of the root causes may vary. It is perhaps revealing that the leadership in the undenominational organization, "Christian Action," and the interdenominational organization of the National Council of Churches and the World Council have on their official board a substantial representation of Congregational Christian leadership.

Recognizing that a changed theological climate had come to prevail on the American scene the denomination approved for study by all of the churches a statement prepared by its Council for Social Action on "The Christian Basis for Social Action." Among other things this affirmation states: "Christian faith requires continual effort to define the basis and the goals for Christian action in society. . . . In the deepest sense all vital issues are spiritual in essence involving personal loyalties and ultimate convictions. . . . Christian Action means the effort to do God's will in every sphere of life."

Recognizing that the leadership of the denomination may have moved too far in advance of the rank and file, a special commission suggested that the Council for Social Action spend more time interpreting to the constituency of the churches the relevance of the Christian faith to the primary social issues of our time; noting that the structure and well-being of the community is a fundamental concern of Christians. Meanwhile, attention has been given such issues as housing, international relations, racial integration, labor-management relations and agricultural policy.

Social Education

As an educationally minded denomination (witness the founding of many colleges, the academies which preceded the public schools and then the support of public education itself) Congregational Christians have kept the social emphasis strong in their literature and their institutional life. In seminaries of Congregational heritage the social emphasis appeared early. These and kindred schools were among the first to include social education in their curricula. Andover, Chicago, Hartford, Oberlin, Pacific School of Religion, Union, Yale, and others, developed departments or programs specializing in social ethics.

In the area of study materials, the Council for Social Action (and also its antecedents) has developed a series of publications, the best known being the journal, *Social Action*. It also prepares "packets" on single major issues for study by churches and groups of interested people. The same can be said of the missionary publications and of *Advance*, the denomination's official journal.

In the forefront of social education and action in Congregational Christian churches have been the women's organizations. Historically most concerned apparently with mission activities these women's groups have turned increasingly to an interpretation of the contemporary scene and major issues of our time. In the more recently emerging laymen's organizations the meaning of the Christian doctrine of *vocation* has been given prominence. Increasing attention to this theme on the part of the National Council of Churches has served to quicken this new emphasis among Congregational laymen and to relate it to a deepened concept of *stewardship*.

Social Research

The social gospel movement gave rise to the necessity for gathering facts relative to the conditions about which the social gospel leadership was concerned. Many of these leaders became amateur or professional sociologists. Many of the pioneers in college departments of sociology were former clergymen. Accurate data about society is a *sine qua non* for any remedial program. It is, therefore, not unexpected that the Congregational Christian denomination has produced a disproportionately large number of the leading religious researchers of America and of those doing fundamental social research relevant to religious life.

Trends in population movements as they affect the life of churches, the impact of social trends upon both urban and rural life, the well-being of various segments of our economy, life histories of religious institutions, and analysis of the role of the clergy in agricultural and industrial areas, are some of the types of research sponsored either by the denomination itself or by agencies with Congregational affiliation. Many of the directors of research in other denominational and interdenominational agencies have been trained under Congregational auspices. The denomination maintains a Department of Research and the leaders of both its urban and rural church departments have been trained in research.

At the national, state, and metropolitan levels, denominational funds have been provided for special studies and in many instances such studies have resulted in a realization on the part of the agencies providing them that a full-time research department is necessary. Metropolitan councils of churches have acquired such departments in this fashion, usually through an association with a theological seminary.

Because attitudinal research is much more expensive than demographic and institutional studies this phase has received less attention. What resources have been available were needed to conduct research where comity arrangements have been at stake and where population mobility has necessitated changes in church location. Possibly the most extensive research activities sponsored by the denomination are those being conducted in the realm of intercultural activities at Fisk University.

Interprofessional and interoccupational relationships among laymen have not been extensive with the exception of a number of conferences for pastors and labor leaders and of management and labor leaders. The denomination itself has as yet done little to establish conferences between pastors and physicians, psychiatrists, social workers, and others. It has, however, at the local level, given encouragement to such gatherings where representatives of all communions and several faiths are involved.

       ✸   ✸   ✸

Co-operation with Other Churches

The Congregational Christian denomination is itself a product of several mergers. As early as 1871, it was officially declared . . . "We desire and purpose to co-operate with all the churches of our Lord Jesus Christ." Subsequent councils reaffirmed this intent in varied phrasing. Absence of parochialism and a deep concern for the total welfare of the community has given rise to the numerous co-operative ventures at the community, the national, and the international level.

A disposition to co-operate with any and all denominations has given rise to active participation in the formation and support of the Federal (now National) Council of Churches, the World Council of Churches, and with state, county, and metropolitan church organizations.

Congregational policy in such matters is substantially reflected in the work of the Church World Service at the international level, the espousal of comity in many types of areas at the national level and the establishment of co-operative parishes at the local level.

Co-operation with Nonsectarian Agencies, Voluntary and Public

The Congregational Christian churches work co-operatively with nonsectarian voluntary agencies because of the denomination's concept of the church's relationship to the community. Such co-operation still leaves something to be desired. Theological seminaries may have failed to make explicit a doctrine of the church in relation to the community which would continue the original and historic concept in congregationalism. The recently emerging profession of social work and the increasing specialization of role for the ministry may have obscured their respective awareness of common ground.

There has been no lack of participation by clergymen in welfare agencies and where social welfare policy is being determined. Throughout all such activities is a conviction that the church serves to sensitize the state in its welfare functions and to help servants of the state and all others understand the meaning of their stewardship of God's order as entrusted to them.

THE DISCIPLES OF CHRIST 4

Of Calvinist derivation and revivalist inspiration, Thomas Campbell, and his son, Alexander, in western Pennsylvania early in the nineteenth century formed a fellowship called Christians, but eventually better known as Disciples of Christ. Joined by others of like persuasion, their plea was for a reunion of the church on the basis of the New Testament. With the Bible as the Disciples' sole rule of faith and life, their polity is congregational, their mind individualistic, and their outlook ecumenical. One of the few made-in-America denominations, the Disciples of Christ, International Convention, has a total membership of nearly two million. The root and expression of social concern in this body is here described by Barton Hunter, executive secretary, Department of Social Welfare, United Christian Missionary Society.

The Basis of Christian Welfare Work

The concern of the Disciples of Christ with the field of social welfare, including both social education and action and what has come to be technically known as social service, is of relatively recent origin. Several factors may be cited to account for this. First, in the early decades of the nineteenth century when the Disciples emerged, few if any of the religious bodies were concerned with social problems as such. Sociology itself had not yet been accepted as a separate discipline in the humanities. There were no specialized social agencies such as we know today. However, along with other frontier Protestant groups such as the Methodists, the Disciples recognized the responsibility of the "local community"—often church centered—to care for its own. Illness, poverty, and drunkenness would often call forth a response of the local church fellowship in terms of money, food, practical nursing and lay counseling which, to a large extent served the purposes of social agencies of a later day.

The Disciples of Christ had their beginnings in the social unrest which followed the American Revolution. They developed among the pioneers who moved westward to take up new lands beyond the Appalachians and in the Mississippi Valley. As pioneers they were intensely individualistic in temperament and were primarily concerned with conquering a new land and laying the foundations for future material and political stability. They were also a rural people and were thus isolated from the worst social problems that confronted the older areas of the nation. The early Disciple leaders

27

were preoccupied with the concept of a "first century New Testament Church" as providing a basis for Christian unity. They were not unmindful of human need, but the immediate task of feeding the hungry and clothing the naked was regarded as the responsibility of individual Christians and local churches and not of the church as a whole.

Disciples were numerically strong in Virginia, Kentucky, Ohio, Indiana, southern Illinois, and Missouri, where passions ran high over the slavery issue. But there were Disciples on both sides of the question and their principal concern was to prevent a break in fellowship between brethren. If in the light of mid-twentieth century thought this seems a strange and incongruous attitude, it should be remembered that a century ago the Disciples of Christ were a new people, a "sect everywhere spoken against," and fighting for the right to be regarded as an orthodox Christian movement. They were theological and philosophical libertarians whose unity was centered not in the creeds but in a simple formula of confession of Jesus Christ as Lord and Savior, and belief in a New Testament pattern of church life with all else regarded as in the realm of human opinion. "Where the Bible speaks, we speak, where the Bible is silent, we are silent," was the characteristic cry of Disciples of Christ.

Social concern then on the part of the Disciples of Christ has been largely the outgrowth of three factors: evangelistic zeal, personal and local group solicitude for individual cases of human need, and a bit of puritanical morality.

In the main it is to be thought of as having been subservient and incidental to other concerns such as Christian unity, personal morality and doctrinal orthodoxy. Work, for example, among the Negroes, the Japanese, and the American Indians in this country began primarily as evangelistic and educational ventures and only later developed into concern for social welfare and social justice, as missionaries and ministers came to know the needs of these peoples.

Interest in social issues, where it has existed to any great extent among the Disciples, has usually been the shadow cast by a few deeply concerned and persuasive leaders. To the extent that there is any agreement and common approach to Christian social welfare work among our people it has been based largely upon the concept of the "lordship of Christ" and the idea that his "example" furnishes a basis for the Christian's daily living.

During the first quarter of the twentieth century the earlier expressions of the social gospel found many listeners among many of the Disciples of Christ and provided considerable basis for concern with social ethics as men attempted to "follow in the footsteps of Jesus" and to seek to express in daily life "the mind of Christ."

More recent theological developments such as neo-orthodoxy

have not greatly affected Disciples' thinking in the field of social welfare, except indirectly. Here it has been largely a matter that the social concern of the ecumenical movement has been accepted by a number of our leaders "as part of" the movement toward Christian unity and, therefore, an emphasis to be considered favorably.

The Motivation for Christian Welfare Work

In the latter part of the nineteenth century, missionaries were sent out to India, China, Japan, and later to other lands and soon found that the care of homeless orphans, medical and hospital services, and educational programs were indispensable to the success of their work. As a consequence a considerable number of institutions dealing with these concerns have been developed, and more recently trends toward union work with other communions in meeting these needs have been characteristic of our movement.

In the homeland the earliest developments in the social field were in relation to Negro education, (beginning about 1875), and among the Southern Highlanders (about 1885). The first home for children was opened in 1889 and the first home for the aged in 1900. In the first two decades of the twentieth century churches and settlement houses were established among the Russians in New York city and Chicago and among the Slovaks in Bayonne, New Jersey, but have now been discontinued. Religious settlement work among Negroes in Indianapolis, Mexicans in San Antonio and Kansas City, and Japanese in Los Angeles (now interracial) are all maintained.

The sense of professional pride and responsibility which serves as a motivating factor in secular social welfare work, has not of course bulked too large in church circles generally. Among Disciples, recognition that professional social service skills are essential has come as a matter of gradual understanding.

The first organized national approach to distinctly social service was made in the formation of a Commission on Social Service by the International Convention in 1911. This commission worked for a number of years under voluntary leadership and with a budget sufficient only for postage and modest office expense. It conceived its task to include social education, social evangelism and social action, as well as social service. In 1919 it was merged with the American Temperance Board, which had been organized in 1907, to form the Board of Temperance and Social Welfare. This organization was merged with The United Christian Missionary Society in 1935, to become its department of Social Welfare.

It is difficult to evaluate the influences which have brought about present day Disciples of Christ concern into social welfare and social reform. In the beginning the motivation was largely that of evangelism with a sense of Christian responsibility for the welfare of the unfortunate. Some of the leaders of the Disciples were powerfully influenced by such European theologians as Harnack, and Schleiermacher. In this country exponents of the social gospel such as Walter Rauschenbusch, Josiah Strong, Graham Taylor, Shailer Mathews and Bishop Francis J. McConnell had a wide following among leaders of the Disciples. The "Social Creed of the Churches," adopted by the Federal Council of the Churches of Christ in America in 1908 had its influence on Disciple thought. Being a Midwestern and rural people in background, the Disciples had a deep sympathy for the plight of the farmers in their struggles to secure for themselves and their families a fairer share of the fruits of their production. The battles of American industrial workers for better wages and working conditions, especially such dramatic struggles as the steel strike of 1919, the coal strike of the early 1920's, and more recently the effort of the automobile workers for better conditions have had their influence upon Disciple thinking.

However, though some of the better trained leadership of the Disciples have felt a strong compulsion to "serve humanity" based upon a well defined concept of "social justice," the interest of the majority of the communion in the social welfare field seems to have largely grown out of the desire to "take care of our own" (as in the case of our homes for the aged) and out of a sense of responsibility for the "poor and needy."

In the last three decades changing social and economic conditions, such as war, financial depression, the plight of millions of refugees, urbanization of life with its consequent juvenile and family disintegration, have all played their part in deepening the concern of Disciples in social problems.

❧   ❧   ❧

Social Service

Social service among the Disciples takes three major forms.

Care of children and of the aged occupies a large place in the social welfare program. In February of 1886, a handful of church people driven by the necessity of finding a home for a deserted child, began the thinking that a year later (March 10, 1887) led to the establishment of the National Benevolent Association. The purpose for which it was chartered was "to help the helpless, to give a home to the homeless, to provide care for the sick and comfort for the distressed."

Seven homes for children and eight for the aged are now maintained by the National Benevolent Association. Each year about 900 children live in the seven NBA Homes because they have lost one or both parents by death, have been victims of broken homes, wards of the juvenile courts, abandoned by their parents, or born out of wedlock.

Six NBA Homes for Aged are entirely supported by the Disciples churches. Faithful members of the Christian Church, past seventy years of age, in a state of health acceptable to the Admissions Committee of the Homes, and without sufficient means to live elsewhere, may become residents of the NBA Homes for Aged.

Two NBA Homes, dedicated in 1949, require partial church support for aged pensioners and retired full-time Christian workers. Four hundred and seventy-seven individuals were served during the year 1953-54.

Social settlement and social center types of institutions are represented among the Disciples by such agencies as Mexican Christian Institute, San Antonio, Texas; Mt. Beulah Christian Center, Edwards, Mississippi; All Peoples Christian Church and Community Center, Los Angeles, California; and Yakima Indian Christian Mission, White Swan, Washington. Flanner House in Indianapolis which began as a project of the Christian Women's Board of Missions has now become a community agency with regard to support and administration.

To some extent our *schools* for Negro youth in the South and for Southern Highlanders in Kentucky must be considered social service institutions. Here the emphasis was not alone upon education but also upon meeting the physical and social needs of the community as well. One of these schools, Southern Christian Institute, has now merged its educational activities with those of Tougaloo College in Mississippi forming a school now jointly sponsored by the Congregationalists and the Disciples.

In addition to the three types of service mentioned above, the Disciples also join with the National Council of Churches in its program of migrant work and are sending a number of young people into this program each year.

Social Action

Certain principles which Disciples of Christ hold as basic to their faith and practice have made them somewhat less effective in the area of social action than otherwise might have been the case. The first of these is their devotion to the right of private interpretation of Scripture which makes agreement on ethical matters difficult. The second is their congregational autonomy which makes co-operative action impossible except where there is substantial agreement. Third, they have from the beginning been dedicated to Christian unity, a concern which by its very nature tends to avoid raising issues. A fourth consideration is the fact that Disciples have no authoritative common voice. The International Convention can speak for itself and in practice is more and more recognized as expressing the conviction of the churches, but in the last analysis its authority is entirely dependent upon individual and congregational acceptance of its judgments. This has meant a varied reaction to social problems.

The same diversity of opinion and practice characterize the Disciples' attitude toward the temperance question. In their earlier history preponderant sentiment favored total abstinence, but this was by no means an attitude universally held among them. It was not until 1907 that steps were taken to organize a temperance board among Disciples of Christ. During the prohibition years the Board of Temperance and Social Welfare was active in support of national prohibition and when the repeal campaign came on, its executive was loaned for a period of nine months to assist the national temperance forces in their efforts to maintain the amendment.

Recently through their official agencies the Disciples have participated more actively in social action. Since 1944 the Disciples of Christ have taken an active part in world relief, contributing over two and one-half million dollars from their "Week of Compassion" funds to Church World Service and similar agencies.

In addition, the Department of Social Welfare receives and distributes many tons of clothing, bedding, hospital supplies, etc., to relief agencies at home and abroad. The department has shared in the program of the Department of State under which qualified German students are brought to the United States for a year of living in American homes and studying in American high schools. It has co-operated in the refugee resettlement program and has sent selected Disciples young people abroad for two-year periods of service on a subsistence basis in war devastated areas under the World Council of Churches. It has a growing work camp program in this country and in Latin America. At the beginning of World War II it became apparent that a number of the Disciples young men would claim conscientious objection under the terms of the Selective Training and Service Act. When the National Service Board for Conscientious Objectors was formed the then executive of the Department of Social Welfare was made a member, a post which he held until his retirement in 1953. The Disciples of Christ have been active in the peace movement. Resolutions dealing with world peace, disarmament, the League of Nations, the United Nations, conscientious objection to war, world relief, human rights, and the like, have been a feature of every International Convention since 1924. The Disciples Peace Fellowship, though never large in membership, has exerted a potent influence upon brotherhood thinking since its organization in 1935.

Social Education

The program of social education among Disciples of Christ normally proceeds through the Division of Christian Education to which the Department of Social Education is related in the person of its director of social education. Through this arrangement social education becomes a normal and natural part of the church school curriculum.

Conferences, workshops, and clinics for discussion of social issues are sponsored by the Department of Social Welfare. Annual seminars at United Nations headquarters serve to keep representatives of the churches aware of what that organization is doing for world peace. A similar group meets annually in Washington as a part of an interdenominational seminar to study our own government and its policies.

Social Action News-Letter, a monthly publication now in its nineteenth year, keeps the churches informed of pertinent developments in the field. Through CAPRA (Christian Action Program Resource Associates) the department makes social education materials available to local churches on a subscription basis at considerable saving in cost.

The department prepares and distributes materials on four social education special days—Race Relations Sunday, Freedom and Democracy Sunday, Labor Sunday, and World Order Sunday.

Social Research

The Disciples of Christ have done little in the field of social research. In 1922, the International Convention authorized a survey of all the brotherhood's agencies and activities, which was published in 1923 under the title, "Survey of Service." The resources, accomplishments and needs of the various agencies were cogently presented in this volume, but objective and critical evaluation of program was largely lacking. Other studies of the various agencies and institutions have by the same token been inadequate. At the present time the Department of Social Welfare is engaged in a careful survey of the practices of our churches and agencies in respect to interracial membership and participation.

*   *   *

Co-operation with Other Churches

Disciples of Christ were among the first to join the Federal Council of the Churches of Christ in America and its successor, the National Council of the Churches of Christ in the USA. They participated in every ecumenical conference preceding the formation of the World Council of Churches and were among the first to apply for membership in that body when it was formed. Through the Department of Social Welfare they have been related to all of the departments in the Division of Christian Life and Work of both councils. Likewise in local situations it is characteristic of Disciples to participate in co-operative ventures in the area of social welfare and social action.

When the Reformed Church in the U. S. (1747) and the Evangelical Synod of North America (1849) merged in 1934, elements of German-Swiss Calvinism and German Lutheranism coalesced. Next to the Bible, the doctrinal standards of the Evangelical and Reformed Church include the Heidelberg Catechism, Luther's Catechism, and the Augsburg-Confession—a combination introduced in 1817 at the formation of the Prussian Union, from which the Evangelical Synod was an emigrant projection. The three-quarters of a million E and R members are most heavily concentrated in the Middle Atlantic and Midwestern states. In theological thought they have made significant contributions. Their concern for people in need is here described by Elmer J. Arndt, of Eden Theological Seminary, Webster Groves, Missouri. His presentation was prepared in consultation with a special committee.

The Basis of and Motivation for Social Welfare Work

This generation of the membership of the Evangelical and Reformed Church rejoices in the heritage it has received not only from the "fathers" of its own institutional beginnings on the American continent but also from other communions, notably the continental churches resulting from the purifying work of the Reformation. Such an acknowledgment of its heritage is indispensable to an understanding of the history of its work in the fields of social service and of social action alike, and its present activities in these two areas of social welfare.

The history of social welfare in the Evangelical and Reformed Church is the story of how a number of leaders and a body (or bodies) of Christian people gave a recognizable (but not easily definable) stamp to their heritage and contemporaneous movements within the churches, first under the necessities, limitations, and opportunities of the American frontier and later of contemporary American culture. The history of social welfare and its present status in the Evangelical and Reformed Church is illuminated when it is set in a larger context. Historically, the developments in this area are an aspect of the Americanization process of German (and German-speaking Swiss) churches on the American frontiers first in Pennsylvania and later in the Midwest. It is part of the story of a synthesis (never so stabilized as to think of itself as completed) of the legacy of Luther, Zwingli, and Calvin, of the unionistic and pietistic movements in Germany, of

34

adaptation to American conditions as they evolved with the expansion and industrialization of the United States, and the vital, creative surge of the Christian spirit as it found embodiment in leaders and constituency.

The basis of our welfare work is the teaching and example of Jesus Christ. Carl J. Scherzer in *The Church and Healing* has expressed the source of the interest of the Church in healing in a way which reflects very well what appears to have been and continues to be the inspiration and authority, not only for the founding of hospitals but also for the whole field of social service. He wrote: "The Church received its interest in the healing arts from Jesus. He not only healed the sick, but, more important, taught love, kindness, consideration, and other virtues which may be summed up in the word 'compassion.' This compassion in the lives of his followers impelled them to be interested in the sick and the suffering. Just as their Lord did what he could to relieve the sick, they, too, would help all in trouble." (pp. 29f.).

Replies from present administrators cite commands of Jesus and his example as the basis of work in the field of social service. One respondent wrote: "Biblical authority and Bible command combined in the development of this work of a children's home. The pure religious concept to 'care for the widows and orphans,' 'inasmuch as ye did it unto the least of these, ye did it unto me' and 'let the little ones come unto me' have been historically used as the basis for this work." Another administrator of an institution for chronic epileptics, mental deficients, and mental seniles, writes: "The place of biblical authority in the development of the sense of responsibility for the work of Emmaus is in the command to 'preach the gospel and heal the sick.' There was a unity in Jesus which made these two one. As Jesus ministered to the mentally ill, the Gadarene and the epileptic boy, we feel that Emmaus work is a special function of the following of the over-all directive to the Church."

Such statements are typical. The emphasis is on the teaching and example of our Lord which is understood as both sufficient and authoritative. Other motives or authority are either subordinated to or included in this basic authority.

The motivation of social service in the Evangelical and Reformed Church is a complex of factors. Of primary significance has been the spirit of service taught by and exemplified in Jesus' own ministry and emphasized as characteristic of the Christian. This motivation was given particular form to meet specific needs: care of German immigrant sick, the absence of provision for orphaned children, the disintegration of social relations in the centers of urban areas, and the like. It is abundantly clear that developments in Germany provided inspiration and models for social service in the earlier periods. Changing social and economic conditions have to a considerable degree influenced the forms of social service, the adaptation of existing forms of service and the programs of social service institutions.

* * *

Social Service

The two denominations which united to form the Evangelical and Reformed Church were both heirs of the Lutheran and Reformed branches of the Reformation and both were initially frontier churches. The Reformed Church in the U.S. began with a ministry to Palatinate Germans who had settled in eastern Pennsylvania in the first half of the eighteenth century. The Evangelical Synod traced its beginnings to a ministry to German immigrants who settled in the area of St. Louis in the second quarter of the nineteenth century. The conditions of the frontier, the continental heritage, the special requirements of the German immigrants, and the interests and outlook of the early leaders combined to produce the resultant characters of the two bodies and, ultimately, the one body.

It is noteworthy that the two denominations which united to form the Evangelical and Reformed Church expressed their concern in the area of social welfare in different ways. The Reformed Church founded schools, colleges, and seminaries. The first "orphans' home" was opened in 1863 in Philadelphia and was followed by the establishment of four others, the last in 1910. One hospital, Fairview Park Hospital, Cleveland, Ohio, founded in 1892 by the Reformed constituency, is now among the ten related to the Evangelical and Reformed Church. Homes for the aged (five in number) were not established until the twentieth century. The Reformed Church established both of the academies and seven of the eight colleges which are now related to the Evangelical and Reformed Church. At the time when the proposed union between the two denominations was under discussion, the Reformed Churches maintained three theological schools. It is appropriate at this point to notice the interest of the Reformed Church in immigrants and immigrant groups. The Board of Home Missions of General Synod appointed a harbor missionary at the port of New York in 1884 and continued that work into the twentieth century. The same board initiated work among Hungarian and Bohemian immigrants, the Volga Germans who emigrated to Nebraska and South Dakota, German immigrants in Saskatchewan and Winnipeg, and Japanese on the Pacific coast.

The constituency of the Evangelical Synod of North America, on the other hand, established children's homes, homes for the aged and hospitals in greater numbers than colleges and seminaries. At the time of the 1934 union, the Evangelical Synod maintained one college and one theological seminary; but its constituency supported five homes for children (the earliest founded in 1858 and all before the close of the century), ten homes for the aged, two homes for epileptics and feeble-minded, and nine hospitals.

Two philanthropic institutions of the early days of the Church Association of the West, the *Kirchenverein des Westens*, which evolved into the Evangelical Synod, owed their inception to the initiative of the pioneer philanthropist, Louis Nollau. One was the Good Samaritan Hospital, established in 1857 to care for the physical and spiritual needs of German patients. The founding of this hospital was inspired by Fliedner's institution at Kaiserswerth, Germany, and the hospital begun (1849) in Pittsburgh by the Lutheran pioneer, William Alfred Passavant.

Nollau in his first report accepted the principle of Passavant that acceptance and treatment of patients would be without distinction of creed, race, nationality, or color. The hospital was conceived as a refuge for the needy, the poor to be treated without charge and all to receive expert medical attention and friendly care. The institution was warmly supported by the people who were members of congregations affiliated with the Church Association of the West, as well as by philanthropically minded people not affiliated with those congregations.

The second institution, the German Protestant Orphans Home, founded in 1858, also owed its inception to Nollau and, like the hospital, was supported by the church paper, the *Friedensbote*, and the constituency of the Church Association. The home was a response to a need—children orphaned by the hardships of frontier life and the cholera epidemics of the period.

These two types of institutions, together with homes for the aged, were representative of the interest of the Evangelical Synod in social welfare. In spite of the early failure among German American evangelicals to follow the lead of the deaconess movement in Germany, the movement did finally achieve a footing in the Evangelical Synod. Nine of the ten hospitals now related to the Evangelical and Reformed Church are still called "Deaconess Hospital," although only one (St. Louis) still has a relatively large number of deaconesses on its staff. This aspect again underscores the influence of German church life and practice just as the influence of Bodelschwingh is discernible in the homes for the feeble-minded and epileptics.

In the twentieth century and presently in the denomination, the interest in higher education, contributed in such a marked degree by the Reformed Church, and the interest in benevolent institutions, contributed by the Evangelical Synod, has not only been maintained but extended. As church-related colleges and hospitals have faced new and difficult problems, the church has increasingly given sympathetic interest and financial support.

Several current trends are presently discernible which reflect a response to present needs. One is the interest in providing homes for the aged, of which nine have been established since 1925. The other has been the establishment of group work programs, especially in urban areas.

In addition to these agencies, there is a strong interest in chaplaincy services, especially in hospitals—an interest obviously connected with the strong interest in church-related hospitals. The interest in hospital chaplaincies includes in a few cases support for a chaplain in municipally supported hospitals.

The church, through local synods and the denominational Board of Christian Education maintains a number of camps and vacation services serving young people and family groups and offering a program of Christian education and recreation.

Some of the social service institutions of the Evangelical and Reformed Church were founded primarily to care for its own children and its own aged; others were founded to care for such children as were without homes, the sick who required attention, and people who needed other forms of service—and always with the conviction that a *spiritual* ministry was of fundamental importance, together with other forms of service offered. While at present a certain priority is accorded to Evangelical and Reformed people in some institutions related to the denomination, it appears that the contemporary emphasis (supported largely by practice) is strongly on service to underprivileged and disadvantaged persons and groups.

The adequate financing and staffing of certain benevolent institutions has posed a difficult problem for the denomination. The problem is especially acute in the case of hospitals. In spite of these and similar difficulties, the present trend of the church in the field of social service appears in the following: First, there is a patient but steady effort to strengthen the ties between the denomination (as represented either in synods or general synod) and the benevolent institutions. The institutions, which in many cases were or are governed by independent boards, are being requested to appoint or admit some board members elected or appointed by the synods. Second, a growing recognition on the part of the denomination of its responsibility to provide adequate financial support. Third, the Commission on Benevolent Institutions is progressively making its influence felt both on the institutions and on the denomination, interpreting the needs and interests of the two to each other. The trend is indicative of a conviction that the agencies of social service can function best when they are controlled by the spirit and presuppositions of the Christian faith and that the Christian spirit is most effective in social service when it employs the best methods and practices in the field of social welfare.

Social Action, Education, and Research

The discussion of social action in the Evangelical and Reformed Church has been postponed to this point to be treated separately, primarily because it has its own special aspects. Social action is itself still a "controversial" matter in some quarters and the subjects it deals with are frequently "controversial" even when there is no controversy on the place of social action in the life of the church. Historically, social action, at least as espousing a *systematic* program to bring the whole of life, including social institutions and group relations, under the discipline of Christian conscience, was a relatively late development in the Evangelical and Reformed Church. Such a program, however, was not a breach with the past, but rather a development of what was latent.

The action authorizing the appointment of a Commission on Social Service (under the Board of National Missions) by the General Synod of the Reformed Church in 1914 and the creation of a Commission on the Common Welfare (later in 1921, a Commission on Christianity and Social Problems) by the General Conference of the Evangelical Synod in 1913 were both directly influenced by the adoption of the "Social Creed of the Churches" by the Federal Council of Churches of Christ. While the "Social Ideals of the Churches" provided the stimulus, both denominations made it quite explicit that the main reason for launching the programs to be undertaken by the Commissions was that the full gospel be preached. That gospel included the social ideals of Christianity which must be proclaimed and lived by the church. Both Commissions were established in response to the implication of divine sovereignty, to study social problems in the light of the teachings of Christ and to discover what needed to be done "to Christianize the present social order."

When the two denominations united in 1934, both had active commissions and the Constitution of the Evangelical and Reformed Church provided for a Commission on Christian Social Action. In the last two decades the work of the Commission has steadily expanded and won increasing respect in the denomination and has received increasing support from the denomination.

The Constitution of the Evangelical and Reformed Church provides: "It shall be the duty of this commission to study the content of the gospel in its bearing on the individual and on society, recommend social action for the church, provide and publish information and literature on social issues, co-operate with other agencies in making the implications of the gospel effective in society, and formulate and promote a social program of the church."

One of the most comprehensive statements prepared by the Commission was "Objectives for Christian Social Action," which was adopted by the General Synod in 1942. Over the years, the Commission has prepared a number of statements on particular issues: "The Church's Teaching on Marriage and Divorce" and "Interfaith Marriage;" on the Church and war, conscientious objectors and peace-time military training; on labor-management relations; on the use of alcohol; and on many specific issues in various fields of social life.

Intercultural relations, especially "race relations," have been a very important concern, indicated by the fact that one of the associate secretaries is designated "associate secretary for race relations."

Besides race relations, and in addition to a well rounded concern for the whole sweep of "life and work," the Commission has been giving emphasis to "the Christian and his daily work" and "religion and public education."

The Commission has sought in its reports, statements, and proposals for action to make clear the Christian principles involved, i.e., to provide a solid biblical and theologically sound ethical basis. It has further recognized that many social problems and issues involve both ethical and technical considerations, and has sought to be both discriminating and informed, as well as sensitive and courageous in dealing with such problems.

The one strikingly productive piece of research conducted by the Commission was an investigation into the labor conditions and personnel practices of the various church-related institutions of the denomination. That study, one may believe, contributed to a marked improvement in the labor practices of the institutions concerned.

* * *

Co-operation with Other Churches

The history and the character of social welfare in the Evangelical and Reformed denomination reflect its history and character as an institution. As an institution, the Evangelical and Reformed Church could be described as a process of union of evangelical Christian missionaries, congregations and groups of congregations composed of immigrants and their descendants from Germany and Switzerland. The Evangelical and Reformed Church is now looking forward to organic union with the Congregational-Christian Churches. The former is itself a union (effected in 1934) of the Evangelical Synod of North America and the Reformed Church in the U.S. And both these constituent bodies of the present church were in turn unions of several elements. The histories of both the Evangelical Synod and the Reformed Church were influenced in their interest in union both by ecclesiastical, theological, and religious developments in European continental protestantism and by the necessities and conditions of the American frontier.

A typical example of modern ecumenical spirit on the part of the Evangelical and Reformed Church is the participation of the denomination in interdenominational programs of work among migrants and the resettlement of displaced persons and refugees. The advantages of a co-operative approach to these issues have been accepted, and loyalty to the principle of co-operation in these areas has been and is strong.

THE FIVE YEARS MEETING OF FRIENDS

Nearly two-thirds of America's 115,000 "Quakers" are joined into a loose confederation of Yearly Meetings known as the Five Years Meeting of Friends. Gaining early prominence in the Middle Colonies, the Friends in America have since exercised growing influence at home and overseas. Best known in our time for their efforts in behalf of peace, as well as through the manifold activities of the American Friends Service Committee (1917), the foundation and extent of their social concern is here set forth by a commission. Appointed by William Merton Scott, executive secretary of the Board of Peace and Social Concerns, its members include David E. Henley, Errol T. Elliott, and the secretary.

The Basis of Christian Welfare Work

"To the Quaker all of life is sacramental" and "all the world is a sanctuary," in the words of two non-Quaker writers of the present day. Hence, it is difficult to isolate the "social welfare" message and work of Friends from their worship on the one hand or from their work-a-day life on the other.

Five Years Meeting Friends, in this regard, are in line, essentially, with British and Philadelphia Friends. Quakers generally base their interest in social welfare on the spirit and teachings of the New Testament, especially as expressed in the life and teachings of Jesus. To early Friends, in the middle of the seventeenth century, as in the *Discipline* of 1834, Christ was the "Divine word, to which the Scriptures bear testimony." These Friends believed that the whole spiritual life grows out of the soul's relationship to God. Whittier, the Quaker poet and social prophet, expressed his "unshaken faith in the one distinctive doctrine of Quakerism—the light within—the immanence of the Divine Spirit in Christianity." The dominant text for this view was, "This is the Light that lighteth every man that cometh into the world."

Friends test social attitudes and programs of action by their belief that, first, there is a God of love and, second, there is "that of God" in every person, regardless of race, nation, or class. Consistency with these two views became their touchstone for daily life. There is, then, no clash between biblical requirements and humanitarian standards. But this kind of religion lifts humanitarian impulses to divine imperatives. That is why Penn came unarmed to make his treaty with the Indians and said to them, "Our object is not to do injury, and thus provoke the Great Spirit, but to do good

—I will consider you as the same flesh and blood with the Christians, and the same as if one man's body were to be divided into two parts."

The dependability of this indwelling, available Spirit of God was expressed by Fox and his followers in 1660 in these words, "the Spirit of Christ, by which we are guided, is not changeable, so as once to command us from a thing of evil, and again to move us to it."

These early Friends believed they were reverting to primitive Christianity when they preached the love of God for all people and when they sought practically to "bring deliverance to the captive" and to soften the lot of the poor, the prisoner, the blind, and the mentally ill.

The Motivation for Christian Welfare Work

The humanitarian work of Friends was a far cry from the "alms-giving" of those among the medieval Christians who disdained the recipient but gave as a means of saving their own souls.

Friends, through their doctrine of the "Inner Light," "that of God within," or "Seed of God," took quite literally the emphasis of Jesus, "I was hungry and ye gave me to eat—I was in prison and ye came unto me." To the sensitive Quaker "that in me that cares is the best that is in me; this is the Godlike bit of me reaching out to the same in you, whoever you are."

This kind of social service relieves, rehabilitates, and reconstructs all of those who thus share the love of God—both the giver and the receiver. This attitude combined elemental sympathy, a "consciousness of kind" (to use a later phrasing), a response to "that of God," and a sense of oneness in Christ.

All of this does not mean that early Friends ignored sin or the sinfulness of man. But it does mean that men—as men, not as a few elect—had within them the capacity for the redemptive and regenerative work of God's love.

Today Five Years Meeting Friends are not equally unaffected by theological movements of the times. Some have accepted uncritically certain elements of neo-orthodoxy, more have accepted from the wider church community an emphasis on an evangelism for the individual, but Quakerism generally is still a balanced blend of the personal and the social, of the inner and the outer, of the mystical and the practical. It is a way of going at life. The two Philadelphia Yearly Meetings, in 1949, gave expression to this in words acceptable to Five Years Meeting Friends: "Jesus taught and exemplified in his life, that love is the highest law and that every individual, of every race and nation, is of supreme worth."

Quaker concern for the souls and the whole lives of people everywhere has been essentially the same for three hundred years, though the channels of action and the specific applications have varied. Creative peace-making, liberty-making, equality-making, all start with an *inner* experience of the peace of Christ, whether expressed in prison reform, liberation of slaves, war relief, mission work, education for all, fair trade, or race relations work.

Early Friends knew the urge both to minister to their own (thousands of their breadwinners often being in prison at once for conscience sake) and to plead for aid for others in their own country and in foreign lands. With the coming of respectability and privilege, Friends have turned their attention more to others. London and Philadelphia have kept more clearly a "sense of society" for themselves while at the same time cultivating a universal outlook. Five Years Meeting Friends, while varying from region to region, have become more "community conscious" and have absorbed more of the prevailing views of their neighbors outside the "Society."

❋   ❋   ❋

Social Service

George Fox's long appeal to the magistrates of London for aid to the hungry, the sick, the blind, and the orphans asked: "How dwelleth the love of God in you. . . . Surely, surely you know not that you are of one mould and blood, that dwell upon the face of the earth." About 1658, he caused to be organized a group of sixty women to care for the sick, the orphans, and others. This was primarily for those of Friends who needed help, but the aid was extended to others. Friends meetings were the occasion for the gathering of hundreds of beggars, and others without food, who waited confidently for the bread which they knew would be coming from the bakers, especially for them. Concern for the poor led to special meetings on their behalf.

Before 1660 Friends were keeping careful records of the needs of the poor and of steps taken to give them aid. By 1698 Friends were formally instructed to aid in establishing workhouses for the poor; and by 1742 the *Discipline* asked, "How are the poor among you provided for and what care is taken for the education of their offspring?"

Jails and prisons were matters of firsthand experience to thousands of Friends. They undertook to relieve the distress of their own and their families and they ministered to other individuals, as well as appealing to the consciences of the authorities to improve the consideration given to such unfortunates.

By 1776, Friends had formed the Philadelphia Society for Relieving Distressed Prisoners. However, the best known movement in this work flowered in the early nineteenth century. Elizabeth Gurney Fry, who at the age of eighteen had started classes for

44

children of the poor, was stirred by eyewitness accounts of jail life. Stephen Grellet of America aroused English Friends to this need. By 1817, an association was formed for the improvement of women's prisons and to provide schools for children in prison. A matron was provided; cleanliness, work, kindness, Christian love, brought results that were startling to the authorities. Yet interest in prison reform has been rather spasmodic in recent Five Years Meeting history.

Early Friends developed an understanding of mental illness ahead of their times. The idea that an insane person was ill rather than evil grew out of their conception of human personality and its divine nature and worth. The best known forerunner of modern care was the York Retreat, started by William Tuke in 1792, which still continues its service.

Friends generally, including the Five Years Meeting, have experienced a revival of interest in the mentally ill in the twentieth century. This has become pronounced since World War II when many Young Friends did their alternate service in mental hospitals. Several have become students of the problem professionally. Some are psychiatrists. Others have led in the national mental health movement and in state programs. The wartime units in the mental hospitals have been replaced by "Institutional Service Units." These are made up of students from colleges, medical schools, and seminaries.

Early Friends were motivated by a strong sense of mission. Their missionary message was universal, to the church and to the unchurched everywhere. About the middle of the nineteenth century the strong inflow of evangelical influences opened up new channels. Before the century was over various Friends groups had started mission work, often educational, in many countries in all continents. This interest brought new life to many Friends meetings at home and directed Friends sympathies to new concerns.

Friends relief work in wartime is a special story. It provided a constructive alternative for young men unable to take part in the war itself. It gave much needed relief to war victims. It provided freedom of action in pioneering with small, pilot projects later to be expanded by others. It returned to Friends a group of dynamic leaders.

During 1864-1865, Friends in Baltimore organized the Baltimore Association for relief, rehabilitation, and agricultural experimentation in the southern states. Their rehabilitation of schools won acclaim from governors and legislators as well as educators.

The well known Quaker star, worn for identification, was used in the Franco-Prussian war relief in 1871 and in the major war relief projects of the present century. Friends pioneering in direct relief, rehabilitation, and reconstruction have always been nonpartisan. They have sought to make their service a ministry of reconciliation. Small in number but with freedom for prompt action, they have developed patterns and methods that might be adapted to the use of others.

Since World War I, Five Years Meeting Friends, along with others, have channeled their service activities increasingly through The American Friends Service Committee. To this agency, organized in 1917, they have contributed their full share of administrators and program directors. Child feeding and other relief in the coal fields, rehabilitation and resettlement projects for the unemployed, urban centers for American Indians, and village assistance in India are among the significant present day projects. Work in the coal fields and the work in India particularly illustrate experiments in Quaker co-operation with the government. This is done with the hope that the strength of the government may be utilized while the warmly personal approach of the private agency is maintained.

Some constituent yearly meetings and the Five Years Meeting are now awakened to the needs of the retired, the aged, and the infirm. Others have developed significant vacation camp programs for children and young people. A few have been designedly interracial. A bold example of service to a needy group was the prompt move of Friends in California, joined by eastern Friends, to aid the "relocated" Nisei Japanese in desert camps in the early 1940's, and to initiate a program for getting college-age youth, and later families, into eastern communities.

Social Action

It is especially difficult to separate Quaker social service from social action. Most of the social service has had as one of its aims the bringing about of social change. Early Friends were ahead of their time in relating these two activities or in combining the two purposes in a single program. In the present century some Friends were quick to see that social service might be done in such a way as to contribute to social action and improvement of the economy.

The problem of slavery presents the clearest case history of Friends having moved from acquiescence or participation in a social evil to its complete eradication from the group and eventually from the larger society.

The first generation of Friends was aware of this evil as had been non-Friends before them. A second stage of opposition saw other more sturdy souls rally to the position of those few saintly spirits such as appeared in 1688 at Germantown, Pennsylvania, to be followed by John Woolman, Anthony Benezet, and others. A third stage saw the leadership of London and Philadelphia gently but firmly helping Virginia and Carolina Friends through to a sense of the requirements of Truth and consistency.

46

Friends first denounced the *purchase* of slaves who had been se-cured by the war method. Then the selling apart of members of the family. Next came all trading in human beings. Finally, the more tardy and hard members were *required* to free and equip their slaves. Then the more conscientious and courageous spirits looked outward and joined the movement to abolish slavery in America.

On the whole, however, Friends accepted or condoned general practice, usually tempering personal dealings with Christian feel-ings. So Friends in North and South have had, in the last few dec-ades, to work through again from sensitivity to consistency on the race question. Practices here have been far from uniform, even in the Five Years Meeting. Some midwestern and western schools and meetings moved this time much earlier and more rapidly than did the eastern communities.

In recent years, The American Friends Service Committee has insisted that all of its student projects must be interracial, and it has played a leading part in working for fair employment practices in such cities as Philadelphia, Washington, Indianapolis, and Los Angeles.

In the quietistic period of Quakerism, Friends attempted to with-draw and keep themselves unharmed by the evils surrounding them. But generally Friends have followed Penn's example of pos-itive action, and today they often quote as a text his saying: "True godliness does not turn men out of the world, but enables them to live better in it, and excites their endeavors to mend it."

Friends at their best test social action generally, whether ac-cepted practice or action designed to change the practice, after the manner of George Walton, who, in 1934, said to a schoolteacher, "We can test all our actions by magnifying them to an interna-tional scale, then seeing whether they look like war or peace; we must not trample upon the minds of the students."

Friends of the Five Years Meeting have not yet developed any striking testimony on the social and economic order. They have been inclined to accept the prevailing economic and political pat-tern in which they lived while endeavoring to promote justice, to ameliorate harsh conditions, to cultivate the middle class personal virtues, and to be sensitive to the requirements of Christian love in business and in the duties of citizenship.

Problems of war, the state, civil liberties, international affairs, the United Nations, military training, migrant labor, labor rela-tions, agriculture—all have had devoted study and action from in-dividual Friends and small groups. The educational work of the American Friends Service Committee has been directed to such problems through work camps, seminars, institutes, and professional study teams.

Since 1943, the Friends Committee on National Legislation has maintained an able staff at Washington to interpret and promote Friends views on legislative events involving great moral and humanitarian issues.

The Five Years Meeting Friends have relied heavily on these two agencies. But, save recently on the issues of race and war, Friends today have not matched the unity of concern and action formerly focused on slavery, intemperance, and war. Contrasted with first generation Friends, the present generation shows the effects of prosperity, respectability, and popularity.

However, the influence of central Quaker beliefs is not gone. Recent world events, better education, the experience of many in the Friends Committee on National Legislation and the American Friends Service Committee—all have brought new life to many parts of the Five Years Meeting. Its new *Discipline*, 1951, went through many conferences and trial editions, all yielding educational results. This edition carries a forceful new section on the social order. It bases its stand on the same approach to life as that of early Friends and closes with these words: "In every social or business relationship Friends should seek diligently and experiment actively to find ways of bringing a social order based on the Christian principles of justice, love, and goodwill" and calls for "penitence for society's sins . . . in carrying on the work of social redemption."

Social Education

Social education among Friends has been largely an indirect education through action projects, mentioned above, and through the studies growing out of such service-motivated action.

Friends, as noted earlier, had from earliest days a strong and sensitive social concern for Truth and consistency. This has been revived in recent years through publications for use in Christian education, in institutes on international affairs, in the Quaker Economists' seminar in 1949, followed by two others, one in 1950 of industrialists and one in 1951 by industrial and labor leaders, and a similar conference in Washington by Quaker farmers and government leaders.

The Friends Committee on National Legislation carries on a program of social education directed on the one hand to the membership and other interested churchmen throughout the country and on the other to the legislators and their committees in Washington. The distinctive features of this program are: first, the high level at which the work is pitched, and second, the *universal concern* as distinct from "special interest" lobbying.

Friends colleges recently have moved into labor-management relations, community dynamics, and technical assistance.

The Five Years Meeting, in 1950, united its "Peace Board" with the Social Order Committee to form the "Board on Peace and Social Concerns." This Board carries on its own program of education and assistance and produces special study manuals on problems of the economic life, rights of conscience, temperance, and other issues.

Social Research

In recent years considerable social research has been done by individual members of the Five Years Meeting of Friends, often in other agencies, or with others in the American Friends Service Committee, the Friends Committee on National Legislation, or Friends colleges.

Russo-American relations, migrant labor, labor-management relations, food surpluses and hunger, the role of Truth in an age of power—these and other topics of vital interest have had serious attention by working groups of adult leaders, either in colleges or one of the committees.

However, Friends research work has reached far beyond the organization itself. For Friends approach to life is more fruitful in producing research-minded men and women than in providing the machinery of social organizations.

*   *   *

Co-operation with Other Churches, and with Nonsectarian Agencies, Voluntary and Public

Ecumenicity and comity, for Friends, can be understood only as part of their history. Friends started out with no thought of becoming a separate sect or denomination of the church, but with the idea of working for new spiritual vitality in the church. Theirs was, they thought, a universal call to spiritual-ethical Christianity.

Opposition drew them together. Both their emphasis on the inwardness of religious experience and on the outwardness of its expression helped to exclude them from the state church and from the nonconformist churches, as well as from interdenominational gatherings which based fellowships on either rites and ceremonies or on intellectual statements of doctrine. Unfortunately, this led to an exclusiveness among later Friends from which some are just now emerging. However, Friends have been ready to co-operate in practical affairs of social service and in this the Five Years Meeting has been at the forefront of Friends groups.

Friends have found co-operation with others most fruitful in relief, relocation, and rehabilitation projects. They co-operated with Jewish groups and with Catholic organizations in work for members of these groups when they were victims of war or of persecution and oppression. This co-operation has taken the form of relief, of aid to refugees, and of community rehabilitation. The last named has been especially striking in postwar community projects in Italy. Work in these areas has often led also to active co-operation with government agencies in this country, with CRALOG in Europe, with LARA in Japan, and with government agencies in Korea, in India, and in Arabia.

Friends are known primarily in many parts of the world for their social service. But the perennial springs of this service of love are to be found at the very heart of their religion. In the words of Clarence E. Pickett, this ministry of reconciling love "is for the Quaker what the sacraments are to others, the outward expression of an inner experience."

THE LUTHERAN CHURCHES 7

When Dutch and Swedish Lutherans and, later, waves of Germans came to the Colonies, the pattern was set for a greater diversity in Lutheranism than in any other Protestant communion in America. Huge nineteenth-century Lutheran influxes from Europe complicated the process of adaptation to the ways of a free society, and magnified sociological as well as theological differences. However, a sense of partnership, already present in colonial times within the communion as well as with other Christians, has gradually been gaining. While America's Lutherans today number about seven million, the European Lutheran migration from which most of them are descended also contributed heavily to other denominations.

Lutheran social concern, traditionally tending toward institutional expression, is rooted via the Reformation in scriptural foundations. The description here given reflects the thinking in the three bodies which are in the National Council of Churches: the United Lutheran Church in America, oldest and largest, with a membership of nearly two and a quarter million; the Augustana Lutheran Church, of Swedish descent, with over one-half million members; and the American Evangelical Lutheran Church, Danish Grundtvigian in background, with about 22,000. Representing these three bodies on a specially appointed commission were Francis Shearer, chairman, Lawrence J. Holt, and Holger P. Jorgensen, Henry J. Whiting, director of the Division of Welfare of the National Lutheran Council, which includes two-thirds of this country's Lutherans, was consultant.

The Basis of Christian Welfare Work

Social concern among Lutherans rests on a biblical foundation and is present in the Confessions of the Lutheran Church. This concern derives its authority from God's full scriptural revelation of which Christ is the center. Concern for the needs of the "neighbor" for whom Christ died is a corporate responsibility of the local and universal church. As the head of the church, Christ is also present in the midst of his people as the living and redeeming Word. "So this is now the mark," wrote Luther, "by which we shall certainly know whether the birth of the Lord Christ is effective in us: If we take upon ourselves the need of our neighbor."

Lutherans agree that their activities in the field of welfare, prompted often by humanitarian impulses, spring ultimately from

51

the faith in Christ that is founded in the Word of God. It is this Word that is authoritative, that gives a confident sense of direction, that sets proper limits to the range of endeavor. This is the sense in which the Augsburg Confession, Luther's Catechism, and the other doctrinal standards in the *Book of Concord* interpret Scripture.

Seen from the standpoint of Christian ethics, Lutheran welfare service is faith active in love, sensitive to the Holy Spirit, and responsive to human need. This is not to imply that all Lutherans have thought through the relation between Christian faith and social service. But it is important to note that in Lutheranism the churches give theological affirmation to this basis.

In Lutheranism, moreover, social service is understood as an activity that should grow out of the theology of the church. This theology centers in the Cross. It sees man, the sinner, in revolt against God. It also sees God reconciling the world to himself in the cross of Christ. For God made his Son "who knew no sin, to be sin for us, that we might become the righteousness of God" (2 Corinthians 5:21).

In baptism individual Christians are "buried with Christ . . . into death, so that as Christ was raised from the dead by the glory of the Father, we too might walk in newness of life" (Romans 6:4). In the Lord's Supper this new life is nourished and strengthened. Over against the reality of God's righteous wrath and the solidarity of mankind in sin, the fellowship in God's forgiving love is sealed in the sacraments, the visible Word. The new covenant, which God has in Christ made with his people, binds them together and sends them forth into the world to do his will. In worship, moreover, the liturgy of the church focuses on these facts of faith, and ever reaffirms the basis of right relationship to God and fellow men. Such relationship, founded on justification by faith in Christ, is then to be evidenced by the good works of Christian love.

Lutherans have often known better than they have done, and they would be quick to admit their own failures, when convicted on the basis of Scripture and of Christ as authority. Amid many changes in theological climate, they have remained fairly constant in their basic emphases. They also suspect that their perennial interest in the Reformation is derived from a desire to live in keeping with the Word of God, and that therefore they have much more of a resource in the Christian faith for the demands of a new day than they have commonly ventured to believe.

The Motivation for Christian Welfare Work

The faith by which Lutherans believe the individual to be brought into proper relation to God is the faith which appropriates the promises of God in the love of his Son. While it is the Law, as St. Paul affirms, that condemns the sinner, it is the gospel—the good news of God's saving love—that forgives sin. With this forgiveness comes a new life in Christ, free from the condemnation deserved as sinner and free for fellowship with God in Christ. Such Christ-given life and liberty is a source of profound gratitude. This gratitude finds expression in praise to God through worship and helpfulness to fellow men in service.

In his well known treatise on *Christian Liberty*, Luther put it this way: "We do not reject good works, . . . we cherish them and teach them as much as possible. . . . Although the Christian is actually free from all works he ought in his liberty to empty [identify] himself, to take upon himself the form of a servant . . . and to serve, help, and in every way deal with his neighbor as he sees that God through Christ has dealt and still deals with himself. . . . I will therefore give myself as a Christ to my neighbor, just as Christ offered himself to me. . . . Each should become, as it were, a Christ to his neighbor."

Lutherans agree that they continually fall short of such lofty motivation. They know the twin evils of relaxing into a work-less faith, or of being tempted into a work-righteous faith. At their best they have tried to steer a middle course. Being wise to the ways of human nature, they also know that their motives may be mixed. Love of God as the supreme motivation is directed outward to love for his creatures. It is the fact that Christ died for all men that opens the way to service among them.

In the so-called Lutheran parts of Europe, especially in Germany and the Scandinavian lands, Lutherans commonly constituted the entire community. While the voluntary support of the needy was encouraged by the church in the Reformation era, the subsequent impoverishment of whole communities during the wars of the seventeenth century set the pattern of a progressive reliance upon government for welfare services. Such aid from above was supplemented by concerned Christians working through voluntary means. The orphanage and other institutions of August Hermann Francke in eighteenth century Halle demonstrated new possibilities of voluntary services. In the nineteenth century these possibilities flowered in a profusion of societies and institutions, voluntarily supported and related co-operatively but not organically with the Lutheran territorial churches. Those who supported such undertakings were moved largely by evangelical piety and humanitarian impulse. In Germany these efforts were known collectively as the Inner Mission.

In various fields of need the institutions seemed to provide the most direct form of service in a rapidly industrializing society. From the point of view of conservative government, such merely remedial service was welcomed. Within this context, reform or

53

social action was open to churchmen only within limits. The clergy, as loyal public servants, were not as free as the social radicals to grapple with the destructive forces in society. In short, European Lutheranism was in many instances the religious aspect of the state, and the church was but one of the areas in which government exerted at least a supervisory function.

In colonial America, and then in the rising republic, Lutherans found themselves in a nascent and booming free society. Here they were a minority. Ever and again newcomers among them had to go through the slow process of adaptation. Language was always an initial barrier. So was poverty. As each was surmounted by some, it separated them from others who had come more recently. Successive constituencies of Lutherans thus formed a diversity of ecclesiastical bodies, of Scandinavian and German and other descent. In each body there early emerged a concern for "our own." This led to the founding of homes, institutions, and other welfare enterprises like those in the old country. Further incentive came from the thoroughly American way of forming and joining societies, and thus satisfying some need in the community.

Commemorations and calamities have had their place in moving Lutherans to service. A prominent example is the quadricentennial of the Reformation in 1917, and World War I. The commemoration encouraged church union, while the calamities of war encouraged partnership in practical service projects. Indeed, it is wartime and postwar needs that led to the formation of the National Lutheran Council in 1918. From it sprang a diversity of overseas services which had favorable effect on domestic welfare also. This helps to account for the fact that much of the welfare work among Lutherans today is inter-Lutheran. This interrrelatedness, for example, has gone farthest in the programs of service to military personnel and to refugees, maintained jointly by the National Lutheran Council and the Lutheran Church-Missouri Synod, the latter carrying on all other work independently, in a similar and extensive social welfare program.

The National Lutheran Council, representing two-thirds of America's Lutherans, consists of eight bodies. Each reflects aspects of inherited differences, and all have names whose similarity confuses many Lutherans and frustrates many others. In the Council these eight bodies have since 1918 experienced a fruitful partnership. The Council, through its Division of Welfare (1939), has provided advisory and consultative service, like surveys or planning, as requested by the various Lutheran bodies. When authorized by its member churches, the Council's Division of Welfare—or other appropriate arm—initiates and guides such special services as the resettlement of refugees or the promotion of aid for churches and peoples overseas.

54

A statement such as this cannot, therefore, be dissociated from the wider context of Lutheran welfare services as a whole. The three churches, whose thought and practices are here reflected, are the only Lutheran bodies in the National Council of Churches. While they are but three of the eight bodies in the National Lutheran Council, their total membership accounts for over half of its numerical strength and spans the years of Lutheran history since colonial times.

The motivation which leads to an over-all organizational pattern has its roots in the local congregation. There, through preaching, teaching, and reaching out to others, Lutheran social concern receives its motives. The members of the congregation are to be concerned for one another's needs. Luther's admonition that parishes maintain a common chest for the support of their own needy has left an impact on his followers. At the local level, when need is dramatized by personal ties and firsthand knowledge, the motivation combines human and divine powers. A homeless child, a helpless widow, a sick worker, a stranded immigrant family, a hapless oldster, on the one hand, and a helpful pastor or resourceful church members, on the other, constitute a partnership of need and service out of which Lutheran institutions and agencies have grown.

Support for such work has come from within a given church body, or, it has cut across lines of Lutheran division wherever a constituency has recognized that certain services are rendered better together than individually. So also the names that designate these services embody elements of motivation. "Inner mission," coined in nineteenth century Germany, emphasizes concern for the renewal of people in need, be that need material or spiritual. The same thought of outgoing concern is expressed in the newer term, "social missions." Elsewhere, the word "charity" has been retained; while in the Midwest and on the Pacific Coast, the word "welfare" has gained favor, especially for inter-Lutheran agencies. Whether it is the Lutheran Inner Mission Society of Baltimore, the Social Missions Society of Illinois, or the Lutheran Welfare Society of Minnesota, whatever the name, the motivation springs from the same basis and proliferates in an extensive combination of services.

* * *

Social Service

Lutheran social services express church-consciousness and church-relatedness. These grow out of an effort to adapt old patterns to the requirements of a free society, in which the dual sense of obligation toward a theological heritage, on the one hand, and a sometimes over-size needy constituency of "our own," on the other, determined the nature and course of service. This is evident from the history and development of agencies in the fields of family and child welfare, health and chaplaincy services, care for the aging, the resettlement of refugees, and the like.

Child welfare was first undertaken by Lutherans in America in 1737 when refugees from Salzburg, resettled in Georgia, set up an asylum for the needy in their midst. A plague of fever in that year had left many orphans who were then cared for at Ebenezer in the manner familiar at Halle, Germany. This first Protestant orphanage in America inspired George Whitefield, leader in the Great Awakening, to found a similar home in Bethesda, near Savannah. The oldest still operative Lutheran agency for children is Emaus Orphan Home (1809) in Middletown, Pennsylvania. Among the many orphanages founded in the nineteenth century was an Augustana home, opened at Red Wing, Minnesota, in 1865, and a Danish home in Chicago begun in 1884.

When in 1905 a Lutheran agency in Minneapolis first provided casework service and foster-home placement, a trend began which has since become dominant in Lutheran child welfare. Today the Lutheran Welfare Society of Minnesota, with a staff of thirty-five professionally trained social workers exemplifies the development of state-wide Lutheran agencies which strive to uphold the standards set by the church, by the state, and by the Child Welfare League of America. While these developments have been most noticeable in the Midwest, older agencies in the East have been revamping their programs to conform to modern requirements. Some of these institutions have undertaken specialized services for predelinquent, emotionally disturbed, and handicapped children. Of the eighty-seven Lutheran agencies providing child care in 1950, twenty-three were supported co-operatively, while fifteen were United Lutheran, twelve Augustana, and two American Evangelical.

Family welfare among Lutherans began with the nonsectarian German societies in the seaboard cities. Henry Melchior Muhlenberg, the organizing genius among the colonial Lutherans, supported the formation of the German Benevolent Society in Philadelphia in 1764, whose special task was to aid immigrants. A decade later he praised a similar society in Charleston, South Carolina, as the "flower and crown" of the Germans there. Elsewhere, local congregations usually did what they could for needy families in the neighborhood.

Church-sponsored help for immigrant families was more effectively developed after 1865 when it took the form of "immigrant missions." New York was the focal point for this activity, which included a bureau of information, lodging, referral to congregations en route, and similar services. Some of the methods of the modern resettlement of refugees have a longer church-related history than is commonly supposed.

The first Lutheran family agency along present day lines was set up in Philadelphia in 1902. Of the nearly forty Lutheran agencies giving family service today the United Lutherans support five, the Augustana one, while twenty-nine are co-operatively conducted by various Lutheran bodies.

Health services among Lutherans have come a long way since Muhlenberg, and other pastors, kept a chest of herb remedies inside the church door. A century later, in 1849, William Alfred Passavant opened the Pittsburgh Infirmary, said to be the first American Protestant Hospital Association. Home mission trail blazer that he was, Passavant was also an "inner mission" pioneer. Besides children's and other institutions, he founded hospitals in Chicago, Milwaukee, and elsewhere, which rendered significant service particularly to new Americans, regardless of race or creed.

Today, with nearly one hundred Lutheran hospitals of various types, from Brooklyn to Portland, and from Minneapolis to San Diego, eleven are Augustana-related, five are United Lutheran, while among the rest, fifty-one are maintained co-operatively by Lutherans in the area. Support for these hospitals comes largely from the local community and in part from the church. Ever since Passavant's day, deaconesses have been on the nursing staff of many of these hospitals, and have helped to give the service a distinctive spiritual character. Lutherans have played an important part in the affairs of the American Protestant Hospital Association.

Service to the aging found its initial advocate among Lutherans when Muhlenberg repeatedly proposed an "economical institute" in behalf of "orphans, superannuated pastors and teachers, and their widows." Not until Passavant's initiative in 1859 did the first Lutheran home for the aged become a reality. This Philadelphia institution is the oldest of more than one hundred and thirty such Lutheran-related homes operative today. Twenty of these are Augustana-managed, twenty-eight United Lutheran, and two American Evangelical. In most homes there is provision for special pastoral care. During the past decade the trend in service to older people has been the inclusion of casework in both resident and nonresident care, and also the introduction of group-work projects.

Special services have found Lutheran support for meeting needs as the times required. Seamen's missions, with residence facilities, were begun by Swedish Lutherans in Boston in 1873, and by Danish Lutherans in New York in 1876, with others following in major ports on both coasts. In 1905 the Lutheran Hospice in Philadelphia became the first in a succession of big-city homes for young people away from home. Improvement of economic conditions and the growth of such facilities as those of the Y.M.C.A. and Y.W.C.A. has shifted interest and support away from hospices.

With the opening of the first Lutheran settlement house in 1906, a new concern for community problems developed. A significant variation of this approach had been the growth of interracial neighborhood programs in Lutheran congregations in New York, Chicago, and other cities.

Beginning with a program in Pittsburgh in 1907, the rehabilitation of unattached men through "industrial missions" has been promoted in major urban centers. For underprivileged children the first "fresh air" camp was opened near New York in 1906. Though there are now only three camps of this type, the extensive camping program of the Lutheran churches across the land provides opportunity for children of various backgrounds. Its emphasis on Bible study and leadership training is an important preventive force in the field of welfare.

Chaplaincy service has taken on new significance among Lutherans as well as other Protestants. Indeed, Lutherans have a tradition of pastoral care that centers in the congregation and forms a central element in pastoral theology. In America Muhlenberg and other pastors left detailed records of their counseling. At its best, such counseling has been shared by mature lay members in the congregations and has helped to sustain the burdened, the tempted, and the suffering.

Pastoral visitation among the sick, the hospitalized, the imprisoned, the mentally ill, and others has a long history. As techniques and services in these fields improved, it became evident that pastoral care could also be much improved. Since the 1930's clinical training for theological students has found growing favor both in relation to the seminaries and to interdenominational programs like the Institute for Pastoral Care, and the Council for Clinical Training. The Lutheran Advisory Council on Pastoral Care, co-operating with the Division of Welfare of the National Lutheran Council, has assisted seminaries and other agencies in setting up training opportunities on the basis of professional standards. Today, with over a hundred specialized chaplaincy services across the nation, Lutherans feel that they are also recovering something of the unfinished Reformation and making it available in a personalized application of the Word and sacraments.

Deaconess work for over a century has highlighted the role of women in Lutheran social service. Passavant's practical inspiration for his philanthropical activities was Theodore Fliedner of Kaiserswerth, on the Rhine. It was Fliedner who, in 1836, had recovered the concept of the women's diaconate as practiced in the early church. He gave it modern form, complete with training for specific service such as nursing, teaching, parish work, undergirded by the security of a motherhouse in sickness and old age. At Passavant's persuasion, Fliedner brought the first four deaconesses to America in 1849. They became the nursing staff at the Pittsburgh

Infirmary. Later, two of them rendered distinguished service under Dorothea Dix in the Civil War. In 1884 the first Lutheran deaconess motherhouse was founded in Philadelphia. Since then nine others have been established in Omaha, Baltimore, Brush, Colorado, and other locations. Today, over 500 deaconesses are serving in Lutheran agencies and congregations. The deaconess work has contributed much to inter-Lutheran co-operation. While its standards of training have been rising, the number of recruits does not supply the demand for service.

Social work as a profession has made a strong impact on Lutheran welfare services. Lutherans maintain no schools of social work, but for years they have offered scholarships in this field, and have made extensive use of professional social workers. Periodic action such as the review and adoption of "Standards for Lutheran Health and Welfare Agencies," with repeated revisions upward, has done much to lift the level of service in the agencies of churches co-operating in the National Lutheran Council. This has had a favorable effect on both the staffs and the governing boards. Through the Lutheran Welfare Conference in America, affiliated with the Council's Division of Welfare, agencies throughout the country keep in touch with each other. Regular regional and national meetings of the Conference aid them in keeping up with developments in social work.

Organization for implementing professional skills and theological requirements has already been noted with regard to the Division of Welfare. The latter has its point of contact in the appropriate boards or commissions in the Council's member churches. The United Lutheran Church, for example, has its Board of Social Missions. Formed in 1938 as a merger of earlier boards and committees, it has a full-time staff in charge of Evangelism, Inner Missions, and Social Action. The Augustana Church has a Commission on Social Missions, while the American Evangelical Lutherans have a committee in this field.

Social Action, Education, and Research

When John H. W. Stuckenberg of Wittenberg College, in Ohio, published his *Christian Sociology* (1880), he sounded a challenge that anticipated many of the emphases of the nascent social gospel. His fellow Lutherans, giving him scant attention, continued about their limited enterprises among immigrants, new settlers and others. Their understanding of action was mainly remedial, although some individuals joined with other Christians in common causes such as temperance, the abolition of slavery, and Sabbath observance. One of these was Samuel Simon Schmucker, president of Gettysburg Seminary (1826-64). Synods, on occasion, became active in social reform. The General Synod, representing the more

Americanized Lutheranism, for a time belonged to the Federal Council of Churches and shared in disseminating the "Social Creed of the Churches." Yet it withdrew from the Council upon joining in the formation of the United Lutheran Church in 1918.

Walter Rauschenbusch, Baptist leader of the social gospel but of Lutheran ancestry, deplored that the Lutherans in general shared so little in the "new social enthusiasm." "Lutherans," he wrote in 1914, "have beautiful institutional charities. . . . [But] American Lutheranism might have rendered a great service to social Christianity in America by transmitting to us the mature results of social experience and thought of the German churches."

On local and state levels Lutherans eventually shouldered duties in social action. One such was Jeremiah Franklin Ohl, who was active in prison reform in Pennsylvania. Elsewhere, especially in the midwestern states, many Lutherans became ardent prohibitionists and influenced legislation. On the national level, the Lutheran Bureau (1917), and subsequently the National Lutheran Council, through its Division of Public Relations and its Washington office, have been involved in social action issues of national and international scope.

Among the Council's member churches, the Board of Social Missions of the United Lutherans in 1947 added a full-time secretary for Social Action. This board has issued statements on current issues such as labor, world order, race relations, mixed marriages, and the family. These have been distributed throughout the church. The Augustana Lutherans have acted similarly through their Commission on Morals and Social Problems.

Social education pervades the materials prepared today for use in the churches. The curricula for Sunday schools, vacation schools, young people's Luther Leagues, weekday Christian education, and catechetical instruction lay stress on relating the Christian faith to social responsibility. Specific forms of service are described and the ways of positive social action indicated. The sixteen Augustana and United Lutheran colleges have sought to sensitize faculty and students to the duties of responsible Christian action. Among the ten theological seminaries in the U.S.A. of the three churches making this report, social ethics appears to receive greater emphasis at Gettysburg and at Augustana in Rock Island. Social missions is a regular part of the curriculum at most of the seminaries, although the literature on this subject is as yet not adequate.

Social research began in a modest way with the rise of the National Lutheran Council. Statistical data on churches and congregations have since become standard publications. In the past two decades community surveys and studies of agencies have been made by consultants of the Division of Welfare. In related areas the Council's Division of American Missions has made state-wide and metropolitan studies basic to the planning of rural and urban programs. For the improvement of specific services the Division of Welfare has undertaken studies in child and family welfare, older people's welfare, chaplaincy, and other areas. Reviews of the whole field have been made in periodic conferences of leaders in church-related welfare.

Alerted by the political and ideological lessons of our time, Lutherans are gaining an appreciation of the place of social action, education, and research in relation to the essentials of Christian responsibility in and for a free society.

Co-operation with Other Churches and Agencies

The most encouraging aspect of co-operation among Lutherans has been the National Lutheran Council. Its eight member churches include: The American Evangelical Lutheran Church (22,000), The American Lutheran Church (850,000), The Augustana Lutheran Church (500,000), The Evangelical Lutheran Church (1,000,000), The Lutheran Free Church (66,000), The Suomi Synod (31,000), The United Evangelical Lutheran Church (54,000), and The United Lutheran Church in America (2,200,000).

The many references already made to Lutheran co-operation in social welfare would be incomplete without mention of at least two major enterprises, both precipitated by World War II. Since 1940 the Council-directed program of Lutheran World Action has raised some $40,000,000 for special needs at home and overseas. Through Lutheran World Relief a like amount in dollar value of foodstuffs, clothing, medicines, and materials has been provided for overseas relief. In part this has been done within the co-operative framework of the Lutheran World Federation (1947), of which the National Lutheran Council is the U.S.A. Committee.

The second major enterprise has been the postwar resettlement of over 35,000 Lutheran refugees and displaced persons. Co-operation has here linked local congregations all over the country in a common responsibility both international and ecumenical in scope. Specially prepared films, like the prize-winning *Answer for Anne,* informed church members of existing needs and ways to help. Scores of local and regional Lutheran agencies made their service available to newcomers for whom tragedy at home made America necessarily the "land of second choice."

Interdenominationally, Lutherans have co-operated in such joint efforts as Church World Service, the Christian Rural Overseas Program, the Council of Relief Agencies Licensed for Operation in Germany, American Relief for Korea, and others. The three churches presenting this statement are members of the National Council of Churches, and take part in the work of its various units, including the Department of Social Welfare. Ecumenically these same three churches are members of the World Council of Churches, and with still other Lutheran churches in America have contributed substantially to ecumenically guided work.

Co-operation with Nonsectarian Agencies, Voluntary and Public

Lutherans are also linked to the wider reaches of responsibility in a free society. For its constituency, the National Lutheran Council's Division of Welfare is active in such organizations as the National Social Welfare Assembly, the Council on Social Work Education, the Child Welfare League of America, the Family Service Association, and others. Locally, Lutheran agencies are expected to be active in their community councils of social welfare, and in state and regional welfare organizations.

Governmental agencies are looked upon by Lutherans as partners. A Lutheran understanding of the separation of church and state does not rule out the reality of partnership in serving people who are both Christians and citizens. Particularly in welfare, Christian and secular social concerns overlap. There a clear differentiation of duties is essential. The church does not intend to interfere with government, and by the same standard Lutherans cherish and defend the freedom which the church derives from God independently of the state.

In a relationship of mutual respect and co-operation between church and state, Lutherans count on governmental agencies to carry out the responsibilities for the establishment of minimum standards for the protection and promotion of well-being among the people. The practice of licensing, for example, is regarded by Lutherans as protection for an agency which adheres to good standards and as a stimulus to those who have not reached this goal.

Lutheran agencies, for the most part, accept the theory that government has the responsibility to purchase services for persons otherwise unable to do so. Yet public assistance seldom covers the full cost of needed services. Even if it did, the church's welfare task is never done, for people's needs are more than material. The basis and motivation of this task is theological and springs from the redeeming gospel of Jesus Christ.

THE METHODIST CHURCH

A relative latecomer on the colonial scene, methodism after 1760 quickly adapted itself to American conditions and made the most of its opportunities. Strong on evangelism, it became what some have called the most typical form of protestantism in this country. Three major branches united in 1939 to constitute The Methodist Church. Its inclusive membership approximates ten million, with strong constituencies in most parts of the country. Methodists acknowledge that they are "unhampered by a strict theology. They lead with their hearts instead of their heads." Their social concern, vocal and practical, is here described by A. Dudley Ward, executive secretary of the Board of Social and Economic Relations, in consultation with a special committee.

The Basis of and Motivation for Christian Welfare Work

The declaration of purpose of the historic Christmas Conference of 1784 in Baltimore, Maryland, was "to reform the continent, and to spread scriptural holiness over these lands." This was interpreted by the leaders of American methodism to mean "that in the democracy of the new world in process of development there was freedom for all; to every man power was available to make his environment, whatever it might be, serve his highest interests."

The American Methodist circuit riders believed in and preached democratic social concepts which contradicted the Old World tradition that social position should be based on "birth, social status, and property." They were no more favorable to the class distinctions of colonial society.

For them all persons, rich and poor, slave and free, were in need of salvation and must exercise mutual responsibility and concern for each other's welfare. Such beliefs and preaching had profound social implications.

The Social Creed of The Methodist Church declares that such social concern had its source in the founder of methodism, John Wesley. "The interest of The Methodist Church in social welfare springs from the labors of John Wesley, who ministered to the physical, intellectual, and social needs of the people to whom he preached the gospel of personal redemption. In our historic position we have followed Christ in laboring to bring the whole of life, with its activities, possessions, and relationships into conformity with the will of God."

The so-called General Rules of the Church have both positive

63

and negative emphases. Illustrative of negative is the following excerpt: "It is therefore expected of all who (belong to the church) that they shall continue to evidence their desire of salvation . . . by doing no harm, by avoiding evil of every kind . . . such as: the taking of the name of God in vain; the profaning of the day of the Lord, either by doing ordinary work therein or by buying or selling; drunkenness, buying or selling spirituous liquors, or drinking them, unless in cases of extreme necessity; slaveholding, buying or selling slaves; fighting, quarreling, brawling, brother going to law with brother, returning evil for evil . . . ; uncharitable or unprofitable conversation, particularly speaking evil of magistrates or ministers; . . . doing what we know is not for the glory of God, as the putting on of gold and costly apparel; . . . softness and needless self-indulgence; . . . borrowing without a probability of paying, or taking up goods without a probability of paying for them."

The positive rules, being the converse of many of these negative rules, have this introduction: "It is expected of all who continue in these societies (the English societies of early methodism) that they shall continue to evidence their desire for salvation. . . . By doing good; by being in every kind merciful after their power; as they have opportunity, doing good of every possible sort and, as far as possible, to all men: To their bodies, of the ability which God giveth, by giving food to the hungry, by clothing the naked, by visiting or helping them that are sick or in prison" (*Doctrines and Discipline of The Methodist Church,* 1952, pp. 34-35, par. 94-96. Referred to hereafter simply as *Discipline*).

By incorporating these general rules into the teaching, preaching, and healing ministry of American methodism, an attempt was made to carry out in the New World the personal and social aspects of the gospel preached and practiced by John Wesley, who was concerned deeply for the well-being of the workers, the aged, the sick, the poor, the education and care of children, and ridding the land of such social evils as slavery.

As Nolan B. Harmon has recently expressed it in *Understanding the Methodist Church:* "The Methodist passion for social justice, so strong today, stems directly from the principle laid down in these General Rules of the Church. Methodism is not, and never has been, the private cultivation of a mere inner spirituality. Rather it is the dynamic outgrowing of the Christian spirit into every area of life where good can be done to the souls and bodies of men. Its aggressive attack upon evil, public and private, caused one writer to describe methodism as an 'invasive encampment upon the field of the world.' " (p. 93).

The mandate for The Methodist Church in social welfare is contained in the *Discipline,* which is the official guide book emanating from the General Conference, the highest legislative body of the church. The Social Creed (Paragraph 2020 of the 1952 *Discipline*) is the official statement on such matters as family, poverty, and unemployment, working conditions and vocational training, social benefit for workers, collective bargaining and right of labor and management to organize, the economic order, rural life, the harmful effects of intoxicants and narcotics, the treatment of crime, discrimination, war and peace, conscientious objectors, and civil rights.

In all of this The Methodist Church is attempting to combine its preaching, its education and action, and its institutions in a concerted effort to bring a positive expression of the concern of Christ and his Church for all conditions of all people everywhere.

        ✺   ✺   ✺

Social Service

Americans suffered severe privations and economic disaster during and following the Revolutionary War, and also prior to and during the War of 1812. Many local churches, particularly in the larger cities, fed hungry and starving people. Circuit riders provided charitable assistance, gave counsel to the distressed and shared in the hardships of the people. It was not unusual for a circuit rider to administer first aid and give medical advice to settlers who were remote from professional medical attention. The circuit riders had to be familiar with simple remedies, and many became proficient in the medical practices characteristic of those days. These services were offered without charge to those in need. The church had circuit riders who were also physicians, for example William Phoebus, James Findlay, John Travis, and Alexander Talley.

        ✺

Early Methodist Interest in Welfare

Prison Reform. The treatment of criminals in early American prisons was harsh and inhuman. Criminal laws were strict and severe. In some institutions prisoners depended (for food and clothing) upon charitable organizations. Members of The Methodist Church, along with persons of other denominations, assumed responsibility for giving some aid to prisoners. There are few indications that extensive prison visitation was carried on by Methodist preachers. Strangely, little interest was expressed in penal reform or crime prevention.

Temperance Reform. The temperance movement was strongly supported in religious circles. American methodism followed closely the Wesleyan tradition of opposition to the manufacture of and indulgence in alcoholic beverages. Although colonial society did not look upon social drinking with disfavor, habitual drunkenness was frowned upon. The widespread use of drink has always been open to severe criticism. No group has been more vocal than the Methodists. Methodist ministers became leaders in the temperance cause. The temperance movement lagged early in the ninteenth century. By the middle of that century it had a revival which paved the way for the intense interest of methodism in anti-alcohol education and the temperance movement, which is centered now in the General Board of Temperance.

The Place of Women in the Church. The attitude of early Methodists toward women taking a prominent place in the church was varied. In general there was a reluctance to accept the idea that women should take a prominent position, except in such things as described by Francis Asbury when he wrote of the women " . . . who have an active part in the spread of the gospel, taking the initiative in opening the family home for preaching, providing overnight accommodations for the circuit riders, offering effective testimonies at love feasts, and as class leaders conducting prayer meetings and teaching groups of women." The women then as today were interested in the missionary program of the church. They took leadership in such things as the temperance and the anti-slavery movements. Methodist women assumed an important role in the establishment of charitable institutions and societies for the aid of children and women.

The Church and Labor. Religious leaders often lent their support to the cause of the increasing number of industrial workers, especially as the trade union movement began to develop. However, for the most part, the advocates of the labor movement were criticized by churchmen. Religious leaders were conspicuously absent from the labor movement. Laborers felt great need for the support of the church and were still receptive to religion. The principles upon which the labor movement was based, freedom, justice, and equality, were the same principles espoused by many circuit riders; yet, the movement remained estranged to a large extent from religious groups. Few Methodist ministers engaged in activities in association with the labor leaders. Thus, during its early life, methodism in America missed an opportunity to lend dynamic influence to a mass of people who were in great need of its guidance and support.

This pattern was changed during the early years of the present century. The General Conference of The Methodist Episcopal Church adopted the Social Creed, which dealt directly with such matters as wages and conditions of labor, and which was sponsored by the Methodist Federation for Social Service. Increasingly leaders of the Church exerted substantial effort on behalf of the laboring man and the trade union movement.

The Church and Segregation. Early American Methodist churches were interracial to a considerable degree. Separate classes for religious instruction were formed for Negro congregants. However, no mention of membership on the basis of race was made officially until 1786.

As methodism grew, the membership both white and Negro increased. The general practice in the churches was to assign a certain section within the meeting house for Negroes. They were accepted as members and participated in communion services along with the other members.

Social segregation, coupled with a feeling that they were not wholeheartedly welcomed in established societies, prompted Negro Methodists to form separate societies. Negro ministers were ordained as deacons. Gradually Negroes formed churches of their own such as the African Methodist Episcopal Church, and the African Methodist Episcopal Church Zion.

Bitter controversy arose over the propriety of slaveholding. The breach between abolitionists and pro-slavery forces widened, and a division was inevitable. Only recently has reunion taken place.

The advance in principle and practice has been substantial. The General Conference of 1952 (Paragraph 2027, *Discipline*, 1952) declared: "Ours is a world church. As such its responsibility is to unite in one fellowship men and women of all races and nations. As Christians we confess ourselves to be children of God, brothers and sisters of Jesus Christ. This being true, there is no place in The Methodist Church for racial discrimination or racial segregation. 'To discriminate against a person solely upon the basis of his race is both unfair and unchristian. Every child of God is entitled to that place in society which he has won by his industry and his character. To deny him that position of honor because of the accident of his birth is neither honest democracy nor good religion.' " (The Episcopal Address, 1952).

Educational Activity. The official attitude of The Methodist Church has always indicated a deep interest in the education of the masses of people. Leaders of the church, such as Asbury, gave verbal encouragement and financial support to schools when public apathy was discouraging. Action by General Conferences from 1792 on caused increased activity by Methodists in establishing schools. The first students in these schools were boys, but co-educational instruction was not long in coming. A considerable number of institutions of higher education have been founded by

Methodists. These institutions faced many financial hardships. Methodist colleges founded from 1820 to 1844 include among many others DePauw University, Randolph-Macon College, Wesleyan University, Emory and Henry Colleges, Allegheny College, Dickinson College, Ohio Wesleyan University, and Northwestern University. There was a growing desire for theological training. Between 1814 and 1860 a number of theological schools were founded. From these beginnings, The Methodist Church has moved into a position of pivotal leadership and extensive involvement on all levels of education.

*

Present Day Methodist Activity in Social Welfare

The modern social program of The Methodist Church can be interpreted along two major but closely interrelated lines; one, the work of institutions for social welfare and education; and two, the program of social education and action being carried on by many agencies of the church. The social work program of The Methodist Church is an integral part of its world-wide missionary program.

The size of The Methodist Church has given rise to a complex organization. Two boards of the church have been given special responsibility for the administration of social welfare institutions. One is the Board of Hospital and Homes, and the other is the Board of Missions.

The Board of Hospitals and Homes. The Board of Hospitals and Homes has " . . . an advisory relationship to Methodist philanthropic interests and institutions, such as hospitals, homes for the aged, homes for children, and homes for youth located in the United States, its territories, and dependencies. . . . " Growing from small roots to its present wide proportions, there are now affiliated with the Board of Hospitals and Homes of The Methodist Church (official standardizing and co-ordinating health and welfare agency of the church) a total of 199 institutions: 73 hospitals, 69 homes for the aged, 49 homes for children, and 8 homes for youth and deaconesses. These institutions are annually caring for 1,147,242 persons, and represent total assets of $289,457,937. Last year 37,980 persons served in these hospitals and homes.

But figures alone do not tell the complete story of the relation of The Methodist Church to health and welfare. More significant is the fact that methodism is a very important part of the national health and welfare program, and is daily exerting a vast influence in the thinking and planning for better facilities and service in the future—for all people.

It is the concern of the Board today that hospitals and homes should offer the strongest, finest care, through Christian personnel. The Golden Cross Society of The Methodist Church gives needed care to the sick, the children, the aged, who could not otherwise care for themselves financially.

The Board of Missions. The Board of Missions has three administrative divisions—National Missions, World Missions, and the Woman's Division of Christian Service. For the purpose of this paper, the Division of National Missions and the Woman's Division are of particular concern. The Division of National Missions consists of a section of National Missions and a section of Church Extension. In the section of National Missions there is a Department of City Work, which is responsible for functioning in cities with a population of ten thousand and over and aids in making surveys in cities with special reference to the religious conditions of foreign speaking, Negro, or other minority groups; the location and adaptation of church buildings, and programs required for needy and congested communities, including the services rendered in connection with the juvenile court cases; the support of rescue missions, and of institutions of relief of the sick and the destitute.

The Department of Town and Country Work serves a similar purpose in rural areas and in towns of population of less than ten thousand, seeking to undergird a co-operative procedure among church and other agencies that are seeking to improve the economic, social, educational, and religious life in town and country areas.

Another department is Good Will Industries, which provides religious, educational, social, and industrial welfare for handicapped and unfortunate people. It is responsible to conduct regional institutes and training activities, to develop people specially trained to help the handicapped. Stores and outlets are operated throughout the country for the sale of merchandise, both donated by the churches and made by the people in the Industry itself.

The Woman's Division of Christian Service, through its Department of Work in Home Fields, maintains a broad program of social work in the United States and Territories, by supporting more than 300 projects including 93 urban social settlements, 8 hospitals, 44 homes for children and young women, 70 town and country social service institutions, and 33 educational institutions plus numerous local church and community social workers.

Recruiting and training of personnel plays a vital part in raising the standards of service rendered by the entire Board.

Social Action and Education

The program of social education and action of The Methodist Church is centered in many general boards, for example, Education, Lay Activities, Missions, particularly in the Woman's Division. Three boards have special designated responsibility in social education and action—Temperance, World Peace, and Social and Economic Relations.

In the Woman's Division there is the Department of Christian Social Relations and Local Church Activities, which has a responsibility to co-ordinate the social action activity of the women's work in the jurisdictional and annual conferences and in the local church societies. The work includes preparation of program material, conducting social action institutes, and providing general leadership in matters of peace, temperance, economics, international affairs, and race relations.

The Board of Temperance is responsible to conduct an intensive educational program with distribution of literature on voluntary total abstinence from all intoxicating beverages and narcotics, to stimulate the observance and enforcement of legal requirements in reference to alcoholic liquors and narcotics, to promote legislation for the control of liquor and narcotics. The Board has a responsibility to counteract the distribution of corrupt and salacious literature, the extension of lotteries and gambling, and in general to sponsor a struggle against social evils and promote high public morals.

The Board of Social and Economic Relations has responsibility in economic life, race relations, and social workers. It is to make available resource material on these matters to help local churches conduct programs of study and action, and to encourage advanced and pioneering projects in social and economic welfare relations.

THE MORAVIAN CHURCH 9

*As the earliest Protestant church with an international organiza-
tion, Moravians first came to the American colonies in 1735. Their
two provinces in the U.S.A. center in Pennsylvania and North Carolina. Evangelical in theology, liturgical in worship, and episcopal
in polity, they have an overseas mission constituency which considerably exceeds in number their nearly 52,000 members in this country. The nature of their social concern is set forth below by F. P.
Stocker, president of the Northern Province, Moravian Church in
America.*

The Basis of and Motivation for Christian Welfare Work

In its historic practice the Moravian Church has always emphasized the headship of Jesus Christ in his Church, the true fellowship of the hearts of believers, the union of brethren one with the
other in Christian witness and service.

The teachings and the example of our Savior concerning fraternal care for the needs of all the children of God are accepted
as binding on the conscience of members of the Moravian Church.
Statements such as those found in Matthew 25:31-46 (the description of the last judgment); Luke 10:25-37 (the good Samaritan);
John 15:5-15 (the vine and the branches); Galatians 6:2; James
1:27; 1 Timothy 5:8, are regarded as patterns of New Testament
teaching which are to guide our Christian relations with those in
need.

*   *   *

Social Service

From its very beginning the Moravian Church has considered it
a duty to see that care is given in the Name of Christ to all members who are in need, or in sickness, or left alone. Accordingly,
there grew up a system of schools, of institutions for the care of
widows and orphans, a system of homes and financial aid for the
aged, especially the aged ministers and missionaries and their
families.

The official statements of the Moravian Church which are still
considered as indicative of the present thinking and practice of
the church are the four which follow.

Results of the General Synod (1889): "Among the reciprocal aid
and service rendered in a Christian congregation is also the administration of alms. Although it may be expected that the more

71

wealthy will readily, from the impulse of their own hearts, bestow on the poorer various gifts which beyond the givers and receivers are known only to Him who seeth in secret, yet, according to the example of the Apostolic Church, a regulated provision for the necessitous is requisite. For this purpose our Poor Funds are established. All persons who are charged with the provision for the poor are not only to preserve the necessary reticence, but also to seek in prayer for tenderness of heart, that they may act in their office after the pattern of our Savior.

"But, in like manner as the care of the poor, it also belongs to the reciprocal aid and service proper in a congregation of Jesus that we, for his sake who 'himself took our infirmities and bare our diseases' (Matthew 8:17), readily and willingly take our share in mutual attendance on the sick. This is probably most easily to be accomplished by the combined efforts of an association for the relief of the sick.

"May He who for our sakes became poor, that we through His poverty might be made rich, go with us into the abodes of the poor and sick, and not only bless our temporal gifts, but let none among us come short of the heavenly blessings obtained for us through His poverty!"

Book of Order: "The granting of temporal relief to the poor and needy must ever form a part of the service rendered by a Christian congregation. Although those of our members who are more favored in temporal things will, known only to Him who seeth in secret, of their own accord feel prompted to remember the needy, yet, according to the example of the Apostolic Church, there should be some definite provision made in every congregation for the relief of the poor. For this purpose funds for the relief of the poor should be established. All almoners are not only to preserve the necessary reticence, but are also to seek in prayer for tenderness of heart, that they may act after the pattern of our Savior.

"It also belongs to the mutual aid and service rendered by every true congregation of the Lord Jesus, when every member, for the sake of him who 'hath borne our griefs and carried our sorrows,' readily and willingly assumes the duty of ministering to the sick and suffering. The care of the sick should not be left to depend entirely on the voluntary impulse of the individual member, but, wherever possible, some definite provision for organized effort in this direction should be made by every congregation."

Journal of the Eastern District Synod (1945): "Resolved, that this Synod go on record as favoring the establishment in the Eastern District of a home for the aged, similar to that at Lake Auburn; and be it further

"Resolved, that this Synod authorize the District Board to appoint a Board of Trustees, consisting of not less than seven nor more than eleven, to secure funds, acquire, establish, and manage such a home."

Book of Order: "This corporation is organized for the purpose of obtaining, establishing, building, maintaining, endowing and carrying on at Lake Auburn, Minnesota, a home for aged men and women; engaging in charitable work in behalf of indigent and helpless people, and providing residences for such persons as may seek rest and quiet." (This statement of purpose also appears in the charter of the Home for the Aged operated by the Eastern District of the Moravian Church.)

Beyond these quotations and explanations, the Moravian Church has not set down a definite statement of its interpretation of the New Testament and the application of its teachings to social welfare.

✿   ✿   ✿

Co-operation with Nonsectarian Agencies, Voluntary and Public

As agencies developed in the United States which received public support, the Moravian Church gradually gave up its system of social welfare. Today all that remains in addition to its schools are the institutions to care for the aged, for the indigent, and for pensioned servants of the church and their widows.

THE PRESBYTERIAN CHURCH, U.S.

Presbyterians in the Southern states form a body distinct from their brethren elsewhere. Their conservative Calvinism, their practice in race relations and other matters, have been conditioned by long experience. Yet they have also been bold to change as need required. The General Assembly in two successive years, 1954 and 1955, reaffirmed the Church's stand against racial segregation as "discrimination which is out of harmony with Christian theology and ethics." Malcolm P. Calhoun, secretary of the Board of Church Extension, here describes the basis of concern and action in social welfare on the part of the approximately 800,000-strong Presbyterian Church, U. S.

The Basis for Christian Welfare Work

The Presbyterian Church in the United States was organized in the year 1861, having withdrawn from the Presbyterian Church in the United States of America at the time of the War between the States. Upon its organization it adopted as its standards the Westminster Confession of Faith together with The Larger Catechism and The Shorter Catechism; also the Form of Government and Discipline of the Presbyterian Church in the United States of America. These standards have their origin in John Calvin. Calvin with Martin Luther represent two types of reformers. While Luther represented a moderate type of reform in matters of government and worship, Calvin favored strict conformity to a biblical pattern of life. John Knox, who sat at the feet of Calvin, based his Book of Discipline upon the studies of his teacher. Presbyterians coming to America brought with them this Book of Discipline and, with amendments from time to time, it has continued to be their guide in matters of church government. Although not written by John Calvin, the Confession of Faith and the Catechisms were produced by a group of divines who are greatly influenced by him.

On June 12, 1643, the Long Parliament in England passed an act entitled "An Ordinance of the Lords and Commons in Parliament for the calling of an Assembly of learned and godly divines and others, to be consulted with by the Parliament, for the settlement of the Government and Liturgy of the Church of England and for the indicating and clearing of the doctrine of the said Church from false aspersions and interpretations." The laborious and tedious work of the divines was finally completed in 1648. These standards were endorsed by the Scottish General Assembly, and in 1729, the old Synod of Philadelphia in its "Adopting Act" adopted the Confession of Faith and The Larger and Shorter Catechisms.

These are the documents of the Presbyterian Church in the United States, all of which are believed to be based upon the teaching of the Holy Scriptures. The individual life as well as the corporate life of church members should conform to the standards indicated in these documents.

The Motivation for Christian Welfare Work

Growing out of Calvin's emphasis upon the sovereignty of God was his respect for the dignity and worth of all people, and his zeal in promoting the welfare of the people in Geneva. John Richard Green, in his history of the English people, thus evaluated the influence of Calvin: "It is in Calvinism that the modern world strikes its roots; for it was Calvinism that first revealed the worth and dignity of man. Called of God, heir of heaven, the trader at his counter, and the digger in his field, suddenly rose into equality with the noble and the king."

The Confession of Faith sees genuine faith as producing the fruit of good works. "These good works done in obedience to God's commandments are the fruits and evidences of a true and lively faith: and by them believers manifest their thankfulness, strengthen their assurance, edify their brethren, adorn the profession of the gospel, stop the mouths of the adversaries, and glorify God, whose workmanship they are, created in Christ Jesus thereunto, that, having their fruit unto holiness, they may have the end, eternal life." In The Larger Catechism, the sum of those commandments which contain our duty to man, is "to love our neighbor as ourselves and to do to others what we would have them do to us."

✷   ✷   ✷

Social Service

In keeping with this basis for concern in social welfare, the Presbyterian Church made special provision for ministering unto the needy by having an elective group whose responsibility would be in this area. These are the deacons. States the Book of Church Order: "To the office of deacon, which is spiritual in nature, should be chosen men of spiritual character, honest repute, exemplary lives, brotherly spirit, warm sympathies, and sound judgment." Provision is made also for the assistance of women in ministering to the needy. "It is often expedient that the Session of a Church should select and appoint godly women of the congregation to assist the deacons in ministering to the sick, to widows, to orphans, to prisoners, and to others who may be in any distress or need." This responsibility for ministering to the welfare of those in need is shared by the various organizations of the church in these days, but it had its beginning with the organization of the church.

The Presbyterian Church in the United States has no central agency in control of institutions for the care of orphans, the sick, the aged and others. This work is done through synods, presbyteries, and local church groups. Activities in the area of social welfare, however, are based upon the foregoing principles and procedures of the church.

Social Action and Education

In 1934, the General Assembly first established a permanent committee on Moral and Social Welfare, but no funds were available for promoting the work of such a committee. Nevertheless, the committee served a useful purpose, acting as a channel for stimulating the conscience of the church. In establishing such a committee the General Assembly declared:

> We believe that the Church in fulfillment of its spiritual function must interpret and present Christ's ideal for the individual and for society, must warn men of the presence of sin, and of its effects in individual life and in the social life, must offer Christ to the individual and to society as the only Revealer of God, and the only Redeemer of mankind, must seek with the spiritual weapons at its disposal to establish his Lordship in the hearts of all men and over every area of human life. . . . The Church cannot rest its efforts until all men, in all nations, are seeking to follow Christ, not only in their individual lives but also in their corporate lives, and to build their economic life, their political life, and their international life on the teaching of Jesus. It cannot rest until Jesus is Lord of all men, and until he is also Lord of all life.

In 1946, the General Assembly, recognizing the challenge of the times, authorized the erection of a Committee on Christian Relations, with a full-time director. This committee took over the duties of the Committee on Moral and Social Welfare. At that time the General Assembly said in part:

> In accordance with Christ's command the Church must also teach men to love their neighbors as themselves, and to do so in every area of life, in the social sphere, as well as in the individual sphere, in the home, in the school and in the Church, in industry and in politics, in racial contacts, and in international affairs. . . . It cannot discharge this part of its responsibility unless it deals with those actual evils in the individual life, and in the social order which threaten man's moral and spiritual development, which hinder the progress of God's kingdom on earth, and which produce needless suffering and distress among the children of men; unless in some

definite and concrete fashion it encourages and stimulates its members to realize the ideals of Christ in their individual lives, in the life of each group of which they are participants and in the total life of the nation. . . .

*   *   *

Co-operation with Other Churches

In 1953, the General Assembly of the Presbyterian Church, U.S., together with the General Assembly of the Presbyterian Church, U.S.A., adopted the following statement: "All human life should be lived in accordance with the principles established by God for the life of men and of nations. This is a tenet of biblical religion. It is also a basic emphasis in our Presbyterian heritage of faith.

"As individuals and as a group Christians are responsible for adjusting their thought and behavior to those everlasting principles of righteousness which God has revealed in Holy Scripture, especially in the Ten Commandments and in the life and teaching of Jesus Christ. It is no less their responsibility as citizens of their nation to seek as far as their influence may extend to bring national life and all the institutions of society into conformity to the moral government of God, and into harmony with the spirit of Jesus Christ.

"Believing in the importance and worth of every person as revealed in Scripture, the Church and each of its members should be concerned with the spiritual implications of this fact for all phases of our common life. Only those social practices are righteous and good which help men and women to fulfill God's desire for them.

"If we as Presbyterians are loyal to that which is most distinctive in our own religious inheritance we shall earnestly assert the relevance of our Christian faith to social relations. We shall survey the life of man in the light of Christ's teachings and example. We shall seek to know and to do the will of God in the concrete situations of everyday life. We shall look to the Church for inspiration, guidance and support in this endeavor."

Co-operation with Nonsectarian Agencies,
Voluntary and Public

In confronting the needs of people one must recognize that much of present day social welfare has become the responsibility of the state. It should be pointed out here that the Presbyterian Church in the United States adheres to the doctrine of separation of church and state. At its first General Assembly the following declaration was made: "The provinces of church and state are perfectly distinct, and the one has no right to usurp the jurisdiction of the other. The state is a natural institute, founded in the constitution of man as moral and social, and designed to realize the idea of justice. *It is the society of rights.* The Church is a supernatural institute, founded in the fact of redemption, and is designed to realize the idea of grace. It is the society of the redeemed. The state aims at social order, the Church at spiritual holiness. The state looks to the visible and outward; the Church is concerned for the invisible and inward. . . . The power of the Church is exclusively spiritual, that of the state includes the exercise of force. The constitution of the Church is a divine revelation; the constitution of the state must be determined by human reason and the course of providential events. *The Church has no right to construct or modify a government for the state, and the state has no right to frame a creed or policy for the Church.* They are as planets moving in different orbits, and, unless each is confined to its own track, the consequences may be as disastrous in the moral world as the collision of different spheres in the world of matter."

Such a declaration was not intended to suggest that the state must therefore be irreligious. On the contrary, the state should be guided by those principles of justice which have been produced by religion. John Calvin in Geneva brought his knowledge of Christian principles to bear upon the life of the community to such an extent that John Knox, his disciple, was moved to declare: "In other places I confess Christ to be truly preached; but manners and religion to be so sincerely reformed, I have not yet seen in any other place beside."

It is this that we as Presbyterians aim to accomplish in our relationship with the state and its voluntary and public social service agencies.

THE PRESBYTERIAN CHURCH, U.S.A. 11

With the Presbytery of Philadelphia (1706) as their organizational beginning, Scotch-Irish settlers had brought presbyterianism to most of the Atlantic seaboard by the opening of the national period. Constituted like the new Republic, the first General Assembly convened in 1789. With emphasis on missionary outreach, a trained ministry, and adherence to the principles of the Westminster Confession, Presbyterians exerted strong influence on America's churches. But issues such as emotional revivalism, slavery, theological conservatism, proved divisive.

The Presbyterian Church in the United States of America—as distinct from its southern sister (above)—is the largest body in its denomination. With the exception of New England and the South, its inclusive membership of over two and one-half million is well distributed across the nation. The basis and development of its work in social welfare is here set forth by a commission of the Board of National Missions, comprising Eugene Carson Blake, Stated Clerk; William P. Shriver, Katherine E. Gladfelter, Clifford J. Earle, John Park Lee, Hermann N. Morse, and Harold H. Baldwin, secretary, Department of City and Industrial Work.

The Basis of Christian Welfare Work

The Presbyterian Church finds its basic authority for all that it does in the Bible as interpreted by the Holy Spirit. Subordinate to that basic standard is the Constitution of the church which contains the Confession of Faith, the Catechisms, the Book of Discipline, and the Directory for the Worship of God. All ruling elders and ministers, at their ordination, receive and adopt the Confession of Faith and Catechisms as containing the System of Doctrine taught in the Holy Scriptures. The Confession of Faith (I, 2), reads: "Under the name of Holy Scripture, or the Word of God written, are now contained all the books of the Old and New Testaments. . . . All which are given by inspiration of God, to be the rule of faith and life."

In the Bible as interpreted by the Confession of Faith and the Catechisms, the Presbyterian Church has found in its doctrine of God the fundamental basis for its social welfare concern. Confession of Faith (II, 1) reads in part: "There is but one only living and true God . . . almighty, most wise, most holy, most free . . . most loving, gracious, merciful, long-suffering, abundant in goodness and truth, forgiving iniquity, transgression, and sin. . . . " It is because of the character of this Sovereign God revealed in Christ, that the Presbyterian Church is committed to its social duties that rise out of the gospel. Question 45 of The Larger Catechism, "How doth Christ execute the office of a king?" is answered in terms that make it clear that his sovereignty is not confined to the ecclesiastical realm, but extends to the whole of life. Question 122 of The Larger Catechism specifically asks, "What is the sum of the six commandments which contain our duty to man?" In the reply, it is specifically stated, "The sum of the six commandments which contain our duty to man, is, to love our neighbor as ourselves, and to do to others what we would have them to do to us."

It must be admitted that in these seventeenth century Standards as confessed by the Presbyterian Church, there is less emphasis on a social gospel than a twentieth century Presbyterian biblical interpretation would likely demand. Nevertheless, it is clear that no reversal or revision of the doctrinal position of the church was necessary in order to emphasize the duties of love and service to man, which have been more central to the gospel than the church sometimes in the past confessed or on the basis of which it acted. The parable of the good Samaritan has remained from the beginning in the gospel, and as it is reread from age to age, it has reinspired the followers of Jesus Christ to express their love for men in ways that transcend the barriers of race, politics and even of religious creed. The parable of the judgment in Matthew 25 has been generally interpreted in the Presbyterian Church to give a basis for the integral place of good works in religion, while the Epistle of James has always in our communion served to correct any tendency to limit the concern of the Church to a vertical relationship to God.

The General Assembly of the church, in deliverances on the implications of the gospel for human well-being, often explicitly relates its judgments to particular teachings of the Scriptures or of the Confession of Faith. It thus makes clear its belief that the Scriptures and the standards of the church require and give warrant for the application of the gospel to considerations affecting social welfare.

The Motivation for Christian Welfare Work

From the earliest frontier until now the Presbyterian Church has found the occasion and inspiration of its social welfare service in the needs of the community. Many forms of practical ministry to need were, in every period, practiced by home missionaries of the church. A very early deliverance of the General Assembly noted, in connection with a certain mission to the Indians, the need to "civilize" them in order to "Christianize" them and therefore authorized instruction in husbandry and other social arts. Schools had an important place in mission activities. William Warren Sweet, noted

American church historian, observed that "the Presbyterian minister in the early West was at least half a school teacher. The popular sentiment in the community compelled him to open a school." There were also early instances of an active concern with problems of health, of child care, and of social justice.

When Sheldon Jackson, pioneer Presbyterian missionary to the Far West, confronted the near starvation of the natives of Alaska, he conceived the idea of importing reindeer from Siberia for breeding, to provide both food and clothing. Sixteen head were landed on the west coast. Congress later made an appropriation, and in successive stages herds approximating a hundred and fifty thousand were built up.

From the middle of the nineteenth century, invention, together with the growth of mining and industry, contributed to the building of the cities and to the increase of immigration, with a backwash on the depopulated rural communities. The churches had a new situation to cope with. Home missions was given a new social meaning. The so-called social gospel was rooted in human need.

Under the leadership of Charles L. Thompson, secretary (1898-1914), the Board of Home Missions took a radical turn. A Workingmen's Department was set up under the direction of Charles Stelzle. Later, as the Department of Church and Labor (1908), a pattern of service was established—noonday shop meetings; workingmen's mass meetings in theaters and halls on Sunday afternoons; a labor press bureau; an exchange of fraternal delegates; conferences of employers and employees. With the co-operation of the Presbytery of New York, "Labor Temple" was opened in a vacated church in New York's most congested area, outstanding features being a Sunday night Open Forum and Labor Temple School pioneered by Will Durant.

To meet the emergent conditions created by the new immigration, a Department of Immigration (1910) was placed under the direction of William P. Shriver, to be later known as the Department of City, Immigrant, and Industrial Work. New York city was its first great experimental area, where the American Parish on the upper East Side was promoted by Norman Thomas. The experience gained in this correlated program of church and social work with bilingual leadership was the inspiration of industrial parish work on the iron mining ranges of Michigan, Wisconsin, and Minnesota.

In directing the Board to establish a Bureau of Social Service to include the Department of Church and Labor (1911), the General Assembly said, "it should study social conditions as they are related to the progress of the kingdom of God and to suggest to the Church practical ways of realizing the social ideals of the gospel." There was no false optimism. Those nearest the situation realized the difficulty of the problems involved. They saw, also, the need of a specially furbished and trained leadership. To this the Board turned its attention. Young ministers were recruited for demonstration parishes in town and country communities. Fellowships were given to seminary graduates of high standing for study abroad at the sources of the new immigration. A two-year graduate course for women in church social work was set up in connection with Teachers College, Columbia University, with field work under supervision.

A business depression with widespread unemployment following World War I roused the social conscience of the churches. The Board of National Missions (1931-1932) created a Standing Committee on Social and Industrial Relations with representation from the Board, its staff and the church-at-large, and with John McDowell as secretary. "All the social and industrial problems of America," the Committee said in its report, 1932, "are problems of human relations and therefore are religious problems. The Church cannot advocate a particular method of dealing with the present economic crisis, but it can test all plans and practices by the spirit of the gospel and it can make clear what ends are desirable in our economic life."

With sixteen million out of work, the 1933 General Assembly urged "all members of our churches to give serious thought to the moral, social and industrial problems, and to avail of opportunities for social service; to bring the sense of justice and righteousness and the sanctity of human personality, which is fundamental in Christianity, to bear upon matters of everyday life in business, in politics, in industry and in society." Subsequent reports urged that "men should be valued by the service they render the community; that the rights of property are conditioned by the functions which its holder is able and willing to perform in behalf of the community."

It should be clear from the foregoing narrative that the Presbyterian home mission enterprise has, from the beginning, made an emphasis on service to human welfare an integral part of its concern. The verbal expression of this concern varied from period to period. The question of relative importance was often debated. But the significance of Christian service to need as an essential aspect of missionary effort was seldom seriously challenged. When the Board of National Missions was established in 1923 as a merger of a number of previous agencies, this was made explicit in the charter of the Board which defined its purpose as "the extension of the gospel of Christ in all its fullness and of his service in all its implications."

It can fairly be said that in the Presbyterian program of home missions the sense of responsibility "to care for our own" has always been balanced by an equal sense of responsibility to minister to underprivileged and disadvantaged groups. Early statements of the General Assembly emphasized the duty to minister to Indians, Negro slaves, and "the poor and those destitute of the means of grace." Much of the history of the development of this program could be written in terms of the response of the church to critical phases of national life. Reference has been made to programs initiated to deal with problems occasioned by immigration, growth of cities, rural deterioration and aspects of industrialization. Similarly, work was undertaken on behalf of Negroes following emancipation, of Orientals on the West Coast, of Mexicans and Spanish-Americans in the Southwest, of Indians and Eskimos in Alaska, of workers in deep-woods logging camps. In most instances these programs have included welfare activities through schools, hospitals, homes, and community centers as well as more conventional forms of religious ministry.

* * *

Social Service

The Presbyterian program of social service activities can be most conveniently treated under three subdivisions: (1) work done under the auspices of minor judicatories, local churches or private Presbyterian groups and related to the denomination as a whole through the Division of Welfare Agencies; this chiefly concerns children's homes, homes for the aged, and hospitals; (2) work done by the Board of National Missions through its Department of Educational and Medical Work; (3) other work of the Board of National Missions and of the synods and presbyteries in association with it.

*

Division of Welfare Agencies

Presbyterians have never waited for official direction to provide loving assistance for those in need around them. Through the past 125 years, children's homes and services, hospitals and nursing homes, and homes and medical facilities for the aged have been established and maintained by presbyteries, synods, local churches, and informal groupings of Presbyterians.

To assure the church that such agencies and institutions, virtually all of them named "Presbyterian," were meeting good standards, to keep the church informed of their activities and needs, and to provide counsel for such institutions, the General Assembly in 1949 established the Division of Welfare Agencies, giving it responsibility for the three types of welfare work noted above (other than projects of the Board of National Missions). For administrative purposes it was attached to the Board of Pensions.

83

At the present time, 77 projects of these three sorts are maintained. These include 13 children's homes and services; 19 hospitals and nursing homes; and 45 homes for the aged. These are in addition to four homes with hospital services maintained by the Board of Pensions for retired ministers, and two homes maintained by the Board of Foreign Missions for retired missionaries.

Oldest of the Presbyterian welfare agencies is the Egenton Home (for girls) in Baltimore, which dates from 1836. The Harper Hospital in Detroit, related to the First Presbyterian Church and founded in 1863, is the oldest of the health agencies, while the Presbyterian Home for Aged Women in New York city is the oldest of homes for the aged, founded in 1869.

Co-operation with other denominations has been evidenced. Two of the children's homes have relations with other Presbyterian bodies. One of the child-placement agencies is an interdenominational service in which our church participates. Two of the hospitals are not officially related to the church but were founded by Presbyterians and have informal relationships with the church. In these, of course, members of other denominations share in the direction. One hospital is officially related to the Presbyterian Church, U.S., the Presbyterian Church, U.S.A., and the Episcopal Church.

Four of the homes for the aged include representatives of other Presbyterian bodies in their management and receive members from any Presbyterian church.

During 1954, Presbyterian children's homes and services, hospitals, nursing homes and out-patient clinics, and homes and services for the aged, including all such facilities operated by the boards, totaled 107.

In addition, thousands of Presbyterians serve as board members and volunteer workers for secular welfare agencies of all kinds across the country.

❖

Department of Educational and Medical Work

The Christian Social Service Work of the Board of National Missions has been, in the main, the responsibility of the women's organizations in the Presbyterian Church, and today's program can best be understood against its historical background.

Around 1800, when church women first began to organize for service, their initial efforts were often the "relief of the poor and the distressed" in local communities. Some societies, however, gave money and sewed for "heathen schools in America," or packed boxes for missionaries and their congregations on the frontier. As the interest of the women grew and their gifts increased, more responsibility was entrusted to them until in 1877 the General As-

84

sembly formally approved educational work in the home missions field "as rapidly as the women's societies should provide the funds."

Mission day schools and a more limited number of boarding schools developed rapidly in communities across the country still without public schools and without other services which the average community now takes for granted. In these schools where the missionary teacher was all things to all people, being ready to go at a moment's notice, according to an early report, "as nurse, physician, minister, friend," many aspects of what would today be considered a social service program were carried on. The initial impetus for this educational work was evangelism, through the teaching of reading so that men, women, and children might read their Bibles and have the word of salvation.

This was also true of the medical program as it began to develop in the 1890's. A number of the early doctors and nurses in such then distant points as Alaska and Puerto Rico performed services of the public health type (though this term was as yet unknown), as they attempted to relieve suffering and to teach the rudiments in the prevention of disease.

Various specialized services were also gradually undertaken by the women of the Presbyterian Church. For some years, beginning in 1896, attention was given to the "increasing stream of immigrants" with the result that "the kindergarten for little children, nurseries for the babies of mothers who work, night schools for the adults, mothers' meetings, Sunday school, etc., and self-planned recreation and other means of social expression" came into being as "forms of effort to help the foreigner." A missionary was placed at Ellis Island, and services, later turned over to the Council of Women for Home Missions, were carried on among the migrants. For a time scholarships were available to young women of foreign extraction who wished to prepare for work among their own people in this country.

Presbyterian women, through their national home missions committee, were also active in social issues. One president of this committee personally called on four presidents during their terms in the White House in connection with the nationwide campaign against the practice of polygamy by the Mormons. Various petitions were sent to presidents and to Congress on behalf of the Indians, and the committee "appealed to the women of the church to wage war against alcoholism, the dissemination of impure literature over the country, the desecration of the Sabbath, and against other issues that tended toward the weakening of Christian influence."

In all of the institutional phase of the home mission program, flexibility of service has been a continuing characteristic. Projects have been turned over to public agencies, discontinued, or reorganized as changing conditions lessened the need for one type of service and opened the door for another. One Christian social center of today, with an unusually fine group work and case-work program, began as a rescue mission. A children's home started as a day school and was then a hospital, while in another community a hospital has recently been discontinued and the building converted into use as a Day Care Center and School of Practical Nursing.

*

Other National Missions Activities

Neighborhood and Community Centers. Neighborhood and community centers have had an important place in the program of the Board for fifty years or more. The movement was initiated by the concern of the church for the welfare of immigrant populations in our cities and included a wide variety of practical welfare services. Many such enterprises are still maintained in industrial centers of the East and Middlewest and as a service to Oriental and Spanish-speaking populations of the West and Southwest. Ordinarily, they function in close co-operation with public welfare agencies. A considerable number of such centers are also maintained in depleted rural areas and in the West Indies.

Institutional Chaplaincy. In 1950, the General Assembly of the Presbyterian Church, U.S.A., instituted a Committee on Institutional Ministry, to be appointed by the Board of National Missions and to function under its direction. This special committee in charge of Institutional Chaplaincy has been functioning in co-operation with the Department of Pastoral Services of the National Council of Churches and seeks to serve the interests and needs of our Presbyterian full and part-time chaplains, together with the giving of counsel to ministers who are interested in entering this field of service. A committee counsellor is provided in the person of the Chaplain of the Denver Presbyterian Hospital.

Jarvie Commonweal Service. This is a program of old-age assistance supported by a special endowment which was transferred to the Board in 1934 by the Jarvie Commonweal Fund, established from an eleven million dollar trust gift by the late James N. Jarvie, formerly a member of the Board. Its purpose is "to offer financial aid and friendly service to elderly folk . . . within the Protestant faith and residing within the Greater New York area," with particular reference to "persons of culture and education . . . who in their declining years found themselves without sufficient means of support." During the past year, 527 persons benefited from grants and service through this program.

Presbyterian Institute of Industrial Relations. This is a training program conducted by the Board in co-operation with McCormick Theological Seminary in Chicago, to prepare men for a more effective ministry in industrial communities. It includes both pre-service and in-service training.

Social Action and Education

Prior to the reorganization of the Boards of the Church in 1923, responsibilities within the field of social education and action were principally carried by the Board of Home Missions and the Board of Temperance and Moral Welfare. The General Assembly in 1936 directed that the welfare interests of these former Boards be combined under a Department of Social Education and Action administratively related to the Board of Christian Education. Provision was made for a committee to include representatives of the Board of National Missions and of the church-at-large; also, for a special Standing Committee of the General Assembly through which the report of the Department would each year be brought to the General Assembly for action. This process has considerably broadened the scope of this program and has made it more responsibly representative of the whole church.

General Trends. Prior to 1930, the social concerns of the Presbyterian Church, as reflected in the General Assembly pronouncements, were oriented rather generally toward those moral issues which produced immediate and direct effects upon persons. For example, a large proportion of the pronouncements during the first quarter of the twentieth century, with some notable exceptions, were directed against "the liquor traffic," prostitution, and tobacco.

A signal exception to this preponderant attention to narrowly moralistic issues can be found in the deliverances in the field of industrial and economic relations. As early as 1910, the Church was urging such things as the safeguarding of working people from harmful conditions of labor, the responsibility on the part of industry for the burdens entailed by industrial accidents, disease, unemployment; the right of employees and employers to organize for collective bargaining, and the abolition of child labor. In 1934 the church came out unequivocally for a system of unemployment insurance, and in 1935 for some kind of system of social security against illness and old age, under Federal and state agencies.

Although the church had pronounced on a large variety of social issues, it was not until 1936 that it gave any large place to a *self-conscious awareness* of the need for "a constructive, co-ordinated, and comprehensive program in terms of definite objectives for the whole field of social welfare." Thereafter, a definite trend away from a moralistic, black and white approach to social welfare and toward a more intelligent attempt to understand and evaluate the social, economic, and political forces in their causes and effects in society, can be noted.

Child Welfare. Since 1934, when the General Assembly advocated vigorous support of the proposed Federal Child Welfare Amendment, consistent support has been given to efforts to secure adequate child labor laws in the states as well as the enforcement of the Fair Labor Standards Act in factories that deal in interstate trade.

In the broad category of what is called "juvenile delinquency" the church has recognized the importance of the influence of both home and community on youth. In 1943, it urged parents, employers, public officials, and all responsible citizens to co-operate with the church in providing adequate care for minor children whose mothers were forced to work. As early as 1937 the General Assembly recognized the need for co-operation between the churches and various character-building youth organizations in the community and urged "the most persistent and united efforts of all who are interested in the character education of youth" to work together to meet the physical, mental, and moral needs of young people. It is possible that what the Church has refrained from doing in the area of "juvenile delinquency" is more significant than what it has done. It has refused to make a simple judgment about the causes of delinquency, to assume that the comic books or the liquor advertisements or any other single force has contributed a major part to juvenile crime. It has therefore also avoided giving simple solutions where no simple solutions seem indicated by an awareness of the complexity of the problem.

Crime and Vice. In 1915, the General Assembly repudiated "the spirit of revenge and retaliation" as a justifiable principle on which to build a penal system and emphasized its interest in the rehabilitation of criminals. It urged Christian employers and other citizens to give encouragement to persons who, "having erred against society and having served their sentences, seek employment." In 1910, the General Assembly endorsed and urged the passage of the Mann Act which made "the white slave traffic" across state lines a Federal offense.

Racial and Cultural Relations. Beginning in 1934, with specific reaffirmation of its historic position of "absolute and unmistakable Christian brotherhood of the races and its witness against color and race prejudice," the General Assembly has repeatedly expressed itself in ever more specific terms against prejudice, discrimination, and segregation in any area of public life.

88

Communications. The first mass communications device which attracted the church's attention was motion pictures, the power of which was recognized as early as 1921 when the General Assembly deplored "the menace of moving picture shows to young people because of films that suggest crime, immorality, etc. . . . We urge our people to co-operate with the widespread movement for better motion pictures."

The early tendency of the church was to think in terms of legal censorship by the Federal Government. However, with the growing concern about free speech and free press which developed in the thirties, this movement toward censorship gradually dwindled away, and the emphasis was upon church and parental education to influence the attendance upon "wholesome" films, as well as the cultivation among children, youth, and adults of critical good taste in the selection of movies. Considerable sentiment and support was voiced by the General Assembly for legislation that would prohibit "block booking and blind selling" of motion pictures.

Social Research

The Board of Home Missions was one of the first of church agencies to pioneer in the field of scientific social research related to the program and work of the church. Studies in the urban and industrial field were made as early as 1910; and from about the same time broad sociological studies of rural counties were made in many sections of the country. With the advent of the Interchurch World Movement, with its very extensive survey program, and later of the Institute of Social and Religious Research, the Board of Home Missions sharply restricted its activities in this field. However, although broad sociological studies were no longer made, research in relation to particular situations or problems was continued.

In the Board of National Missions, the Departments of City and Industrial Work and of Town and Country Church Work have continued a program of survey and research within their respective fields. The Board now also maintains an Office of Field Survey with two full-time staff workers. While much of the work of this office is directed toward problems of church location, program, relationships and over-all strategy, the staff are also available for specific studies of particular enterprises and services, at least some of which relate to social welfare activities.

❊   ❊   ❊

Co-operation with Other Churches

The Board of Home Missions had a prominent part in the organization of the Home Missions Council and was thereafter active in all its work. Similarly, the Presbyterian Church, both through its Boards and its ecclesiastical units, has given convinced support to interdenominational agencies, state and local as well as general. The general sentiment of the Presbyterian Church is almost uniformly favorable to the fullest possible measure of co-operation with other Protestant churches.

Most local co-operative projects developed in recent years have been in some way related to this organized co-operative movement. In a limited number of instances particular enterprises or services have been undertaken in co-operation with other church bodies. Co-operation in local projects with Roman Catholic or Jewish agencies has been rare.

Co-operation with Nonsectarian Agencies, Voluntary and Public

The denomination's historic policy on the matter of nonsectarian co-operation has emphasized the following points:

First, not to accept any subsidies from public funds.

Second, to stimulate and assist the development of public or private agencies to meet common health, educational, and welfare needs.

Third, to seek to equal or exceed accepted standards in all educational, health, or welfare services maintained by the Board.

Fourth, to participate in such studies or conferences as seek to develop public understanding or improve performance or open new avenues of service.

Fifth, as regards those services which are clearly recognized as a public responsibility, to seek to transfer projects to public or private support where possible, except where there is clearly involved some "plus value" of religious service.

THE PROTESTANT EPISCOPAL CHURCH

Anglicanism was influential in colonial society. By 1789 it had evolved into the Protestant Episcopal Church, independent of formal ties with England, and complete with an American episcopate. Today its inclusive membership nears two and three-quarters millions. Its 105 dioceses cover the U.S.A. and reach beyond. The Book of Common Prayer and other bonds link Episcopalians to the global Anglican communion. Strongest in the Eastern states, Episcopalians have shared leadership in applying Christian faith to social problems. This concern for the community as a whole is elaborated in the following paper prepared by Almon R. Pepper, director of the Department of Christian Social Relations.

The Basis of Christian Welfare Work

Official recognition that social welfare is an integral part of the mission of the Episcopal Church was given at the General Convention of 1919 in canons establishing the National Council of the Protestant Episcopal Church:

> The Presiding Bishop and the National Council as hereinafter constituted shall have charge of the unification, development, and prosecution of the Missionary, Educational, and Social Work of the Church, of which work the Presiding Bishop shall be the executive head.

Antecedent to the establishment of the National Council, the General Convention had authorized several commissions on labor and social problems; dioceses, parishes, and groups of Episcopalians had established social agencies; twelve dioceses had commissions on social service; and several unofficial associations of Episcopalians had banded themselves together to express their interests in the welfare of working people.

Basic to this concern about welfare work in the Episcopal Church is the life, work, and teachings of Jesus as set forth in the Bible, and as understood by generations of Christians in various social, cultural, political, and economic situations throughout the Christian era. The authority is basically Christological, but it has been bolstered by other influences, such as humanitarianism and democracy. Because the authority is in Christ, every Christian has the right and responsibility to speak and act according to his best judgment on any welfare problem. The same is true for congregations of Episcopalians and for the General Convention operating democratically. There is reason to believe that when General Con-

91

vention has stated a position, this influences the thought and action of the individual member or congregation of the local church.

While the basic social responsibility of the Christian and of the church has never been forgotten, there have been times of lagging and narrowing of interests. At such times, changing theological emphases, such as the Tractarian Movement, the social gospel emphasis, and currently, the ecumenical movement, have played a part in reviving social concerns within the Episcopal Church.

The Motivation for Christian Welfare Work

Motivation is seldom simple. In the Episcopal Church, the motivation for welfare work would seem to be a combination of several broad factors: the life, work, and teachings of Jesus; the doctrine of the Christian Church, especially that of the Incarnation; and the traditions and practices of the Church of England and their development in the United States.

The life and teachings of Christ have provided the basic motivation for the social welfare concern of Christians. "He came that we might have life and have it more abundantly." Of various defined services to men, he said, "Inasmuch as ye have done it unto one of the least of these my brethren, ye have done it unto me." Pure religion is described by one of his immediate followers as "visiting the fatherless and widows." The Sermon on the Mount and the total recorded words and work of Christ are full of direct or implied responsibility for the welfare of men. He healed the sick, gave sight to the blind, cast out devils, fed the hungry, visited prisoners, drove money-changers out of the temple, condemned evil doers, especially those who caused children to "stumble," and he rejoiced that the poor had the gospel preached to them. He opposed injustice in high places and set an example of the healing powers of understanding, forgiveness, and love.

In the doctrines of the Christian Church as they were developed out of the life and work of Jesus, two would seem to have had an abiding influence on the beliefs and practices of Episcopalians and of other Christians. The doctrine of the Incarnation: that God, through his Son, became Man has dignified the worth of every man and, therefore, made man and man's mental, moral, physical, and social welfare a matter of proper concern for every Christian and for the Christian Church. The sacramental principle of life: that material things can be used for spiritual purposes and are the necessary substance of the spirit, has also been an important part of the impelling force behind the social welfare program of the church. Good works along with Faith have their proper place in seeking after salvation.

The Episcopal Church, as it developed in this country, drew heavily upon its antecedents in the British Isles. The *Book of Com-*

92

mon Prayer in its liturgical practice catches up into corporate worship many specific aspects of men's personal and social welfare, and by implication these include all of life. Worship is related to life, and what we pray for we have a responsibility to do something about.

A tradition in the Anglican Church is that the parish church should have a pastoral relationship to every aspect of life within its parish boundary. Thus the parish churches related themselves to public and private agencies in the secular community, as well as those operated under ecclesiastical auspices. The Episcopal Church has continued this heritage of concern expressed by both clergy and laity. During the early part of the nineteenth century it was not unusual for an Episcopal bishop or parish priest to preach a sermon about some human need, or to bring such a need to the attention of his congregation with the expectation that some service would be organized. Members of the laity, of their own accord, were also quite capable of recognizing a need and organizing a general community service. In many instances clergy and laity also caused local government to assume greater responsibility for the needs of people.

Services for the care of the aged have usually been provided solely for members of the Episcopal Church, but most other services were founded for the general needs of underprivileged individuals and groups. In some instances the motivation was Christian humanitarianism, and in others a combination of this and missionary zeal. A recent history of a children's agency, celebrating its centennial, reports: "So profound was his entreaty (the rector's), so Christlike his 'spirit of active, comprehensive, and practical charity,' that several members of his parish, banding themselves into a small Society, made systematic arrangements for clothing the children of the poor in order to bring them under the influence of Sunday school instruction." It is noted that the practice of sending chaplains to public hospitals and prisons which began over one hundred years ago, was and is a generalized Christian service with little thought of enlarging the membership of the particular church.

Today, as a matter of principle and practicality, an increasing number of churchmen accept the increased assumption of responsibility being taken by tax supported agencies. They see less reason for the church as such to organize or support similar services for the general welfare, but do recognize that certain skills and insights are of value to people in all levels of social and economic circumstances. This may cause the parishes and dioceses of the Episcopal Church to develop more generalized counseling and referral services for the needs of its own people. But on basic Christian grounds, the individual Christian and the Church must always keep closely related to the healing of body, soul, mind, and of society, lest relatedness to life be altogether lost.

*   *   *

Social Service

Listings in the national office, based upon reports from the agencies and dioceses, show that the following organized social services are at present related to the Episcopal Church in the United States and overseas. Some of these services are units of larger agencies, but most of them are single operations.

Homes and services for the aged	67
Hospitals and convalescent homes (11)	65
Congregate care for children and youth	49
Youth counseling services	16
Family counseling services	8
Settlements and community centers	23
Seamen's services	7
Chaplains' service (City Missions)	23
Residences and shelters	14
Services to the blind	2
Agencies making grants for child care	6

In addition to these local social service agencies, the National Council's Department of Christian Social Relations has three Divisions: Health and Welfare Services, Christian Citizenship, and Urban Industrial Church Work; and the Committee on World Relief and Church Co-operation, which also administers the program for resettlement of refugees. Two national agencies, the Episcopal Service for Youth, Inc., and the Church Association for Seamen's Work, Inc., federate and serve their member agencies. The National Board of the Woman's Auxiliary to the National Council has its own committee of Christian Social Relations, whose executive is a staff associate of the national Department of Christian Social Relations.

Throughout the church there are eighty-seven diocesan departments of Christian social relations and an equivalent number of committees in the diocesan Woman's Auxiliaries. Twenty of the diocesan departments have full-time or part-time executives. An unknown number of parishes employ social workers, provide chaplaincy service to public and private institutions, and conduct group activities in their parish houses. Stimulated by the national Home Department, several dioceses and parishes work among migrants and, on a regional basis, provide chaplaincy service to the deaf. The Episcopal Church participates fully in the relief and rehabilitation program of Church World Service and the World Council of

Churches and expects to exceed its goal of resettling 1,500 family units of refugees under the present Refugee Resettlement Act.

The needs of people and a strong sense of pastoral and civic responsibility were the chief reasons for the Episcopal Church and its members to enter these fields of service with a program which began early in the nineteenth century and continues to the present time. Several policies or attitudes show themselves. One holds that it is the business of the church to initiate social services and then turn them over to other auspices for continuing operation. Another is the more deep-seated conviction that certain services must be a continuing function of the church because it has distinctive contributions to make. A third attitude is based upon the belief that modern democracy, through tax support and community-wide voluntary association of citizens, has the responsibility, the ability, and the necessary resources to operate the needed social services, and that the present day responsibility of the Christian is to support these services and make sure that they are administered with justice and equality.

Common to all these attitudes is the certainty that, in some way or other, the Christian and the church must retain a vital and active concern for the healing of men's bodies, minds, and spirits.

Social Action

Social action, defined as direct efforts at social reform or social justice, has not often been taken by the Episcopal Church through its official and general bodies. Prior to 1900, social reform efforts were limited to the action of influential bishops and other clergymen, and to unofficial social education and action groups composed of Episcopalians. Since 1900, there have been occasional direct efforts by general church bodies, such as the General Convention, and by the National Council formed in 1919. In addition, diocesan social service bodies, the number of which grew rapidly around 1913, have sought, from time to time, to influence local and state public policy and programs, and have participated in certain social reform efforts.

The General Convention of 1901 created a Commission on the Relations of Capital and Labor, to promote industrial peace, and since that time has concerned itself with a variety of social issues, including the following: temperance and prohibition, traffic in narcotics, child labor and migrant workers, social justice for minority groups, slum clearance, religious and ethical teaching in public schools, tax support for sectarian schools, censorship of movies and salacious literature, social security, various programs designed to promote international peace, disarmament, war profits, military training for youth, prison reform, and world relief and resettlement of refugees.

General Convention and the National Council have relied chiefly on an educational approach to social action, with little disposition to promote causes or single goal reform movements. Interest and activity have in the past been greatest in the fields of economic and international relations, and the objectives have been to encourage churchmen as individuals to pusue certain goals, and to influence public policy both directly and indirectly. A characteristic of the Episcopal Church approach has been the co-ordination and integration of social service and social action efforts and programs.

Unofficial channels for social action have been individual bishops and other clergy, parish groups, and certain voluntary associations of Episcopalians, such as the Church Association for the Advancement of the Interests of Labor (1887-1926); the Christian Social Union (1894-1913); and the Church League for Industrial Democracy, now the Episcopal League for Social Action (1919 to date). Indirectly, the Church has also acted through its participation in the Federal Council of Churches, and the National Council of the Churches of Christ in the U.S.A.

In 1951-52 a national survey of social action conducted by the National Council's Department of Christian Social Relations revealed limited activity on the part of dioceses and parishes even on those subjects on which General Convention had taken a stand, and a desire for leadership programs. As a result, General Convention authorized the development of a Division of Social Education and Community Action, renamed Christian Citizenship, in the Department of Christian Social Relations. Thus, the National Council, which is the executive body between the triennial meetings of General Convention, is prepared to give more effective leadership to this phase of the church's program.

Many diocesan departments have developed committees on Christian citizenship and are preparing themselves for community action. Some dioceses by themselves or in co-operation with other dioceses in their state had already taken action supporting changes in the marriage and divorce laws of their state and on matters such as gambling, bingo, and prison reform. Some parishes have taken leadership in housing reform and rental practices, and both parishes and dioceses have joined with local and state councils of churches on similar matters. As a result of the Division's research and analysis of the immediate results of the Supreme Court's decision on public school segregation in 1954, the National Council itself took a stand supporting the decision as "just, right, and necessary," commended action to the whole church, and requested follow-up reports from diocesan and other church bodies.

There is reason to believe that this type of activity is on the increase in parishes and dioceses of the church.

Social Education

Any sharp distinction between social education, defined as a process for making church people sensitive and responsive to social problems, and social action, tends to be artificial and without useful meaning. This is especially true in the Episcopal Church where education has been seen as a necessary and vital form of action.

The most widespread and common expression of social concern in the Episcopal Church is in its liturgy as set forth in the *Book of Common Prayer*. This expression may be found in the Order of Worship for Morning and Evening Prayer, the Order for Celebration of the Holy Communion, the Offices of Instruction, and the many special prayers set forth for Congress; the state legislatures; courts of justice; for a variety of economic concerns; for social justice and the welfare of families; and a general intercession for working people, sound industry, fair wages, wise government, good schools, and all handicapped persons. The hymns of the church also express wide and definite social concerns.

Social concern and education on social questions have their place in preaching, the church schools, parochial and regional study groups, summer schools, lectures and forums, courses in theological schools, and at special institutes for church workers. Their most formal expression is through the educational and action programs of the Woman's Auxiliary and the Youth Department, the recommended study projects of the Department of Christian Social Relations, and the church school curriculum. The full utilization of these channels of education is yet to be realized.

Sporadic interest has been shown in the Christian concept of vocation, and new impetus was given to the subject by participation in the 1952 Conference on the Christian and His Daily Work conducted by the National Council of the Churches of Christ in the U.S.A. Since then, the Division of Christian Citizenship has helped several dioceses and parishes to hold conferences on the subject.

Currently, in addition to the question of desegregation, the subjects being given widest attention are delinquency, problems of the aged, alcoholism, and the problems and tensions of urban life.

From the rise of the organized labor movement in the 1880's to the beginning of World War II, the voluntary unofficial Episcopal social action groups were undoubtedly the most effective single factor in bringing about greater sensitivity and responsiveness on the part of the church and churchmen. Perhaps the most striking result of activity and influence is the fact that much of what was once pioneering is now the official program of the church.

Social Research

Social research, defined as "the systematic gathering, analysis, synthesis, and interpretation of demonstrable information by scientific procedures," is only having its beginning in the Episcopal Church. Perhaps only one project meets this test: a study of social education and action programs of the church and an opinion poll on social issues conducted by the executive of the Division of Christian Citizenship in 1952. Judged by less stringent test, various other social research projects are conducted in the fields of rural and urban church strategy, and in surveys of social service institutions and agencies. For surveys of general church strategy, the National Council developed a Division on Research and Field Study. Foundation grants have made research and demonstration projects possible under the auspices of the Divisions of Rural Work, and Urban-Industrial Church Work. Surveys of social service agencies, or the need for them, are made by the Division of Health and Welfare Services.

Interprofessional consultations and studies have been rather common throughout the church over the past twenty-five years. In a variety of settings, clergy have studied and explored areas of common concern with social workers, psychiatrists, sociologists, lawyers, leaders of management and labor, and other professions. Local guilds or associations of some of these professions have been organized.

*   *   *

Co-operation with Other Churches

Ideally, social welfare services are as broadly social as possible in their organization, sponsorship, support and purposes, as well as in the range of people served. The social welfare services of the churches have produced co-operation more readily than in most other fields of common Christian concern. Even so, the development has been the product only of the past half century. The Episcopal Church was slow in its co-operation except for the activities of some parish churches and dioceses. This co-operation has usually been with councils of churches locally and nationally, rather than with particular denominations. In the social services there has been co-operation in providing chaplains' services to public institutions, in centralized referral services, and in work among migrants, the resettlement of refugees and world relief.

At the national level, co-operation with the predecessor or the National Council of the Churches of Christ in the U.S.A. showed itself comparatively early in social education, social action and research through the approved participation of the national Department of Christian Social Relations. Some dioceses of the church were founding members or early participants in local councils of churches. The response of the membership of the church to this co-operation has been varied; but since 1940, when the Episcopal

Church became an official member of what is now the National Council of the Churches of Christ in the U.S.A., there has been great increase in the church's readiness to co-operate with other churches and local councils of churches.

In general, the Episcopal Church has been ready to counsel and advise the Roman Catholic and Jewish agencies, and in some instances it has been able to carry on co-operative or co-ordinated services and actions with them.

Co-operation with Nonsectarian Agencies, Voluntary and Public

The Episcopal Church and its members have a traditional readiness to co-operate with general community agencies, both public and private. An impartial study of the religious affiliation of board members of these agencies, made about two decades ago, showed Episcopalians in the lead among such membership. A large number of the laity of the church have chosen social work as their vocation, have prepared for it, and serve readily in nonsectarian as well as church agencies.

Since 1921, the national Department of Christian Social Relations has been an associate member of the National Conference of Social Work, participating in all its activities and maintaining its own booth and exhibit. At least fifteen of the clergy of the Episcopal Church are graduates in sociology, criminology, psychology, and allied fields. A large number of the clergy has taken full or part courses at the several schools of clinical training in pastoral work, and at the Yale School of Alcohol Studies.

All of this participation is encouraged on the basis that the church and its people must be related to this important phase of life and should be prepared to do so in the best way possible. The church is not the sole agency of healing or goodwill, and a readiness to co-operate with and participate in all agencies contributes to the general welfare and provides additional resources to the full ministry of the church.

Clergy and laity alike are encouraged to serve as volunteers on boards, committees, and the services of agencies. Scholarship assistance is provided clergy and laity, both at home and abroad, for graduate training in the several helping professions. The social service agencies of the Church are encouraged to seek membership in such standard setting organizations as the Child Welfare League of America, and the National Federation of Settlements and Community Centers; to join local councils of social agencies; and to meet the standards required for licensing by the state departments of welfare.

Conferences and training institutes are planned for encouraging all of this co-operation. In a free society the social agencies of the church, the state, and the general community should co-operate to the greatest possible extent, for the welfare of men and for the common good.

Dutch Calvinism has been represented in this country in organized form since 1628. Later immigration in the colonial period as well as substantial gains in the nineteenth century centered the strength of this communion in the Hudson Valley and in Michigan, with significant extensions into other areas, including the far West. Incorporated in 1819, the Reformed Church in America adopted its present title in 1867. Its present membership is about 200,000. While the work of the Reformed Church in social welfare is highly decentralized, its attitude on this subject is here portrayed by D. Ivan Dykstra, of Hope College, Holland, Michigan, in consultation with a special committee.

The Basis of Christian Welfare Work

The position of the Reformed churches on social issues is somewhat complicated by the fact that, small though it is, the communion has varied considerably, notably in the eastern and midwestern areas. This difference is largely understandable in terms of its history, the eastern section of the church tracing its origin to the early American immigrations from the Netherlands for the most part, and the midwestern predominantly to a major immigration occurring around the middle of the last century. The eastern section, for sociological reasons and because of its greater antiquity, has been understandably more responsive to typical American influences and is, by and large, thoroughly integrated in American culture. The midwestern section has in the main represented a considerably more conservative temperament, even though the ultra-conservative portion of the nineteenth century immigration soon separated itself to form the Christian Reformed Church.

The situation in the church has, however, not remained static, particularly during the past twenty-five years. The net effect of those years has been a growing cohesiveness in the church, though this has not taken place in a uniform way or without explosive tensions' developing along the way. Factors tending to assure the continuation of this tendency toward cohesiveness are a greater exchange of personnel between the sections; increased planning, particularly in education, on a church-wide scale; and the amalgamation which is taking place particularly through the colleges which enroll student bodies from all parts of the church in the same school.

On the part of the eastern section of the church there has been an intensified search for and achievement of a greater depth in its conception of Christianity, as compared with the relatively easy-going adaptation to American culture which at one time characterized it, along with so many of the American communions. This search is but a part of a general deepening of the awareness of what authentic Christianity means on the part of American Christendom, stimulated both by the trying circumstances of depression and war and by direct contact with continental theology. In the Reformed Church the appeal for deeper comprehension was abetted by the fact that her traditional orientation is strongly theological and biblical. Furthermore, the eastern section of the church could not but be impressed by the fact that, wide as were its differences from the West, the latter was showing a certain kind of vitality against which it was difficult to argue and which, in however modified a form, could well be emulated.

The trends in the eastern section of the church are no less important than those in the West, where the picture is, however, more complex and more revealing. Where the eastern section possessed a rather natural humanitarian interest in the social and ethical aspects of Christianity from which it then seeks to move to a more emphatically biblical-Christian base, the western section could begin with a strong theological orientation and an exceptionally strong missionary interest. This theology is Calvinistic, and is authoritatively expressed in the Belgic Confession, the Heidelberg Catechism, and the Canons of the Synod of Dort. The key concept in this theology is that of divine predestination, interpreted as a determinism not only of ends but of means, and as a predestination of some to eternal life and of others, in justice, to perdition. The church is the gathering of the elect members of the new covenant. The salvation of the elect, based upon the divine election and the gift of perseverance, is eternally assured. Faith, the fear of God, sorrow for sin, and a zeal for righteousness constitute the basis for one's recognition of being elected to salvation. The goal of life is to reveal the character which was bestowed by the divine grace, but innocence and purity of life are themselves the gifts of God through the sanctifying Spirit.

From this theology certain implications are drawn, though the picture is complicated by the difficulty of estimating just how much of what is presumably inferred from the theology is consciously and explicitly inferred and how much has developed through a thoughtless accommodation to an existing social and political milieu. Some things can be said with a good deal of confidence about the social and political positions of this Calvinistic conservatism. The *first* is that the thinking of the church has been shaped as much as anything by a lurking fear of even a semblance of "work-righteousness," certainly more by this than by the idea that all suffering and hardship must be passively accepted as ordained by God. This fear is a natural concomitant of a desire to maintain a high degree of theological purity.

The *second* is that the heavy emphasis has been on the individual's relationship with God. This is the obvious conclusion from the understanding of salvation as a gracious reconciliation between a man and God through Christ, the bestowal of a new relationship of sonship, and the new birth.

The *third* is that, when Christian action *is* thought of, it is likely to be ecclesiastical rather than social, and where "social" action is endorsed it will tend to capture support to the extent that it will clearly contribute to the interests of the church as institution. The Reformed churches have shown exceptional energy in prosecuting the work of the church and particularly in missionary activity, while there is an underlying current of feeling that any social emphasis would constitute a rivalry to this kind of action.

The *fourth* is a rather natural corollary of the powerful sense of being a covenant people, bound not only to God but to one another: social concern will express itself much more naturally for members of the group than for those outside. For all its emphasis on covenant, however, it is probably true that the social concern for those in the group is a simpler humanitarian one, the implications of the covenant not having been explicitly mastered. Sometimes there is an interesting lack of distinction between the nationalist group feeling and the church group feeling. An exceptionally spontaneous response was given to the needs of the Dutch people in the Netherlands during and after the war and during the flood disasters of a few years ago. The needs of other national groups have not aroused nearly the same interest. There is a traditional ready charity for members of the churches. For all the avowals of social equality of races, there has been so far relatively little disposition favoring interracial churches; but a mission among the Negro people in Alabama receives enthusiastic support, because it is "ours."

On specific issues, the dominating positions are not hard to define. Love of political democracy is strong and is a reflection of a democratic polity vigorously adhered to since the Reformation battle against a hierarchical church. The traditional attitude toward war and peace is that peace is, of course, desirable and according to the will of God, and will at length be established by supernatural intervention. But in the meantime the biblical predictions of war are taken to mean that war is inevitable. What is more, since war is part of God's judgment upon the nations, there is a danger that in working for the elimination of war one may hamper God's freedom to exercise his judgments. In regard to the state, there is vigorous defense of the liberty of the church from state interference, but at the same time the natural response is a rather uncritical patriotism, growing in part out of the established-church tradition of the Netherlands and the recollection that the life of the Reformed communion was tied up intimately with the rise of the nation-state. In economic matters, there is staunch support for a traditional capitalism, and the Reformed Church is by and large lagging behind the development of secular American political thought in the direction of a state that is increasingly a welfare state. This outlook has its roots in the concept of the austere virtues of thrift, selflessness, hard work, readiness to accept whatever God has ordained for one, and a sense of personal independence and economic self-reliance. By contending that what is virtuous for us is also virtuous for others, this complex of virtues becomes the basis for a rather unquestioned endorsement of free enterprise capitalism. In the main, labor unions are looked upon with suspicion as corporations are not. There is a strong emphasis on personal virtue, which is somewhat thrown out of focus by a practical identification of virtue with refusal to participate in many amusements.

The Motivation for Christian Welfare Work

This massive outlook has undergone and is undergoing some shifts. A fairly static social outlook which had opposed the appeal to government did begin to fall apart under the pressures of the depression, particularly in the rural areas. A rather smug "holding what we have" attitude, rooted in the idea of a select covenant people, gave way in the late thirties and since to an aggressive church-expansion attitude. This could capitalize on the already powerful missionary impulse of the churches, but this had always been more appealing when aimed at "the heathen" in foreign lands. The war had a complex effect. On the one hand, it was an aid to the break-up of a lingering provincialism and on the other, because the vitality of the Reformed Church looked good in comparison, contact with other groups tended to confirm its own high estimate of itself as a church. At the same time and under the pressure of an undercurrent of insecurity, both on the part of the churches over against secular society and of this church over against other churches, the church moved in the direction of sharpening the distinction between the secular world and the church, and became involved in a rather desperate and not always clearheaded effort to beat every other growing church organization at its own game. Sometimes the church in the process has stepped out of character and pulled in the direction of a sentimental kind of evangelism or a tightly knit sectarianism.

The present is witnessing the development of a more sober understanding of and appreciation for the church's peculiar heritage, without returning to the coldly complacent theologism and ecclesiasticism of an earlier time. What prompts this development is a matter of some speculation. Part of it is due to a belated recog-

104

nition of the quick bankruptcy of a sentimental kind of evangelism, part of it to an awareness of the indefensibility of a sectarian provincialism, part to a growing confidence that American churches have moved significantly and safely away from the enervating liberalisms of a couple of decades ago—especially in their readiness to face up to the real dimensions of human sin and the need of a salvation wrought only by God in Christ, and to face the Bible with a new seriousness. This has made possible for the Reformed churches a larger and less conscience-smitten participation in the ecumenical movement, first in the form of the National Council of Churches, and more confidently in the World Alliance of Presbyterians and Reformed Churches. Most revealing of all is the growing sense of congenial participation in the World Council of Churches, with the latter's intent to set itself emphatically under the command of God in Jesus Christ; its emphasis not only on the American flair for organization and applied Christian ethics, but also on the continental enthusiasm for a fresh Bible-centered theology; and the passion for evangelism and missions which it receives from the younger churches of the world. In these respects the World Council is found to be echoing in a live sense, precisely the key points which have characterized the authentic traditions of the Reformed churches.

The Reformed Church will develop its most significant social concern not on the basis of a simple humanitarianism but only to the extent that this concern becomes a clear mandate of the Scriptures. But there is growing unrest over the simple interpretation of Scriptures as containing a more or less mechanical set of rules to follow, for it is discovered that those rules are not unequivocal and can become playthings in the hands of special interests. There is a growing sense of a need to set oneself really under the command of Scripture, which calls for a deeper apprehension of Scripture as embodying neither such a simple set of moral and social rules nor a set of proof texts which may be manipulated to sanction and enforce a closed and static system of theology, but as embodying a fundamental conception of God and his relation to church and world which will clarify the inference that God's men have a calling to fulfill in making God's will known for all of life and in laboring in a dedicated manner to accomplish it. When it becomes clear that election does not mean election to inaction but to action in obedience to God, that the the divine concern extends not merely to the fellowship of believers but to those outside as well, and that this concern is not merely for an other-worldly bliss but also for the most comprehensive well-being of man here and now —then, without hesitation and uneasiness, the Reformed churches will commit themselves with their characteristic vigor to the task of serving the divine purposes in the social sphere.

THE SEVENTH DAY BAPTIST
GENERAL CONFERENCE

Adhering to Saturday as the Sabbath, the Seventh Day Baptists formed their first congregation on this side of the Atlantic in Rhode Island in 1671. Spreading eventually into some thirty states, they are said to have conveyed seventh-day teaching to ten other religious groups in America, including the Seventh Day Adventists. With a whole membership of about 6,300, their influence has been relatively greater than their numbers. In the following statement, Albert N. Rogers, acting dean of the Alfred University School of Theology, describes the involvement of the Seventh Day Baptist General Conference in social welfare.

The Basis of Christian Welfare Work

Seventh Day Baptist churches emerged with the revival of Sabbath-keeping in England and Wales in the early seventeenth century. Transplanted later in Rhode Island and Connecticut, they followed the frontier westward from the Atlantic seaboard, and their General Conference was formed in 1802. Cherishing always "liberty of thought as an essential condition for the guidance of the Holy Spirit" (as the Introduction to the Statement of Belief puts it), and practicing a congregational form of polity, they have had no binding creed but rather an *Exposé of Faith and Practice,* more recently revised as a *Statement of Belief.* While the Bible has always been regarded as the guide in matters of faith and practice, the right and duty of individual interpretation has been insisted upon.

In accepting Christian baptism it has been the purpose of Seventh Day Baptists to follow the commands and teachings of their Lord as fully as possible, and these have been recognized as dealing with both the individual's life and his relation to his neighbors. Educational and missionary work have resulted at home and abroad. But the basis for their social concern has been more than the pursuit of specific commissions of Christ, for the individual believer's relationship to Christ has been made strong. "What a Friend We Have in Jesus" is a commonly used Communion hymn. The basis, then, for their social concerns is both biblical and humanitarian.

The Seventh Day Baptist minister is called to preach the gospel as he sees it. He is responsible to the local congregation, but it is fully accepted that his primary allegiance is to his Lord, as was that of prophets and priests before him. When differences have arisen on social questions the privileges of disagreement and persuasion have usually been granted. Formal action by a local church, by an association, or by the General Conference is regarded as the majority opinion of the members present, and the right of minorities to hold a variant view is freely admitted. The executive secretary of the General Conference is a layman, and a layman was deliberately chosen to avoid the possibility of theological pressures from the Conference being placed in any way upon the ministry.

Educational institutions have been the chief arm of the churches in aiding individuals to discharge their duties as Christians. Academies sprang up under their influence and three colleges grew to maturity. Seventh Day Baptist influence was in direct proportion to the number and quality of Seventh Day Baptist people related to each one. But the principle of free fellowship subscribed to by the more democratic churches prevented both administrative and creedal domination. With individuals regarded as the free agents of God neither the policies of the churches, nor those of educational institutions, can be dictated by a central agency; but they must be worked out in pragmatic fashion by devoted, likeminded individual people.

The Motivation for Christian Welfare Work

For Seventh Day Baptists the motivation of welfare work has been that of duty. "We believe," they affirmed in a "Statement of Belief" (1937), "that man has moral responsibility, and was created for divine sonship and human fellowship . . . that the local church is a community of Christ's followers organized for fellowship and service, practicing and proclaiming common convictions . . . and that it is through these agencies (evangelism, missions, and religious education) that the church must promote Christianity throughout the world and in all human relationships."

It must be admitted, however, that the most successful programs of church extension have been those based on colonies or off-shoots of older bodies, as the frontier moved westward, and those carried on in different racial groups, i.e., the Chinese in and near Shanghai, the East Indians in Jamaica and British Guiana, and the Africans in Nyasaland. There has been considerable reluctance to proselytize from other established religious bodies.

Several instances of readiness to care "for our own" are on record, such as the relief of Union soldiers in the Civil War, the defense of church members persecuted under Pennsylvania blue laws of the nineteenth century, and the relief of civilians through the Seventh Day Baptist churches in Germany after World War II. Local needs which could be known firsthand have found a quick and sympathetic response, and general approval has been given to such interchurch programs as Near East Relief, the Church Committee on Overseas Relief and Reconstruction, and Church World Service.

❋ ❋ ❋

Social Service

A few instances are recorded of efforts to provide congenial homes "for our own" in connection with the Chicago Exposition of 1893, and in the land development periods of California, Florida, and Texas. These were not completely altruistic, of course, and met with only a limited response.

The Sabbath-keeping principle adhered to by our people has made the five-day week of the teaching profession attractive to many, and this in turn has led many of our members into positions of community leadership.

Social Action

Seventh Day Baptists have been responsive to social ideals through their history and have participated in the broad social movements of the times. Foreign missions have had generous support from them since the 1840's, and they shared in the abolition movement, nearly ostracizing one church in West Virginia where slaveholding was to some extent condoned. They have frowned upon the use of intoxicants in any form and supported actively the Prohibition movement. A less militant attitude has prevailed against the use of tobacco, but ministers and deacons are generally not expected to use it.

The General Conference in 1918 affirmed its support of the Allied cause and the loyalty of its people to the United States government. Military service has been considered as a duty, however unpleasant, although individual pacifists have been regarded with some tolerance and a conference committee to counsel with them was set up during World War II paralleling another committee which enlisted chaplains and a third which attempted to aid men in the ranks with their problems of Sabbath-keeping under military routine.

It should be noted that the belief in a seventh-day Sabbath has been a constant factor in social action programs of the churches. An example of this is seen in the Fouke School maintained for Seventh Day Baptist families and their neighbors in southern Arkansas from 1900 to 1926, to which qualified young people from the churches went as teachers for a year or two—or more—at some sacrifice. Also, this belief has prevented Seventh Day Baptist delegates from supporting the moves that have occasionally been made in interdenominational bodies to increase the legal recognition of Sunday as a day of Christian observance. Some opposition to calendar reform has been voiced on similar grounds.

108

Social Education

Seventh Day Baptists have always desired an educated ministry, and a broad background of training as well as experience has been considered desirable for preachers. Their ministers have studied in the leading seminaries, as well as in the one theological school maintained by the denomination. A certain percentage have embraced the fundamentalist position, while a majority have held either a liberal or a middle-of-the-road theology. Their preaching emphases have not been markedly different from those made in most Protestant pulpits, and have reflected social issues of the times.

Bible study is a deep interest among the Seventh Day Baptist people and is organized and maintained in some places where churches have not yet been formed. The International Uniform Lessons have been used for more than a generation, as prepared from outlines by Seventh Day Baptist editors. Lay leadership is generally found in the Sabbath schools which gives them an indigenous character. A national Board of Christian Education prepares some materials and offers guidance in methods and organization. Youth conferences and camps have been quite popular and effective for a quarter century, both on a regional and national basis.

The oldest publication extant is a weekly magazine, *The Sabbath Recorder,* devoted to general topics as well as to discussion of denominational beliefs and interests. Its subscription lists include perhaps one-third of the members' families, and it is regarded as the organ of most of the boards and agencies operating in the denomination. Numerous other publications, printed or mimeographed, reflect the various special interests of individuals and groups.

A distinctive form of social education among Seventh Day Baptists derives, again, from their Seventh-day Sabbath practice. The General Conference has set up a vocational committee which through the years has attempted to find, with varying degrees of success, employment for church members which will permit their Sabbath observance. Local custom prompts some commercial and industrial firms not controlled by Seventh Day Baptists to follow an established community pattern by closing Saturdays and opening Sundays. The concept of vocation is seen to include Sabbath observance as well as conformity to high ethical standards, but it should be added that there is a marked absence of legalism in the matter which permits members to work when duty to others or unusual circumstances seem to justify.

Social Research

Little has been done by Seventh Day Baptists in the field of social research beyond occasional studies that have been carried on in the preparation of student theses in the School of Theology. The Seventh Day Baptist Historical Society has carried on research in its particular field with respect to the development of churches and movements in the denomination.

At least two special committees have studied phases of the denominational life under tension due to the fundamentalist-modernist controversy. In each case reports were issued which indicate an honest difference of opinion that could not be resolved by persuasion and must therefore be respected under the basic principles of the Seventh Day Baptist belief.

The ministers of the denomination hold an anual conference for study and fellowship to which representatives of other professions have been invited several times as resource leaders.

❖   ❖   ❖

Co-operation with Other Churches

Individual members of our churches helped to found the Federal Council of the Churches of Christ in America, and the World Council of Churches. Official participation in these, and in the International Council of Religious Education, was voted by the Seventh Day Baptist General Conference as each body emerged. On one or two occasions when this ecumenical participation was questioned, the majority has been clearly shown to favor it. On a local basis, also, the readiness to co-operate in interchurch programs for social betterment has been almost universal among our people.

Co-operation with Nonsectarian Agencies,
Voluntary and Public

It has been the usual practice of Seventh Day Baptists to carry on whatever welfare work seemed needed through public or nonsectarian agencies. Often, in fact, members of our churches have held public offices carrying considerable responsibility in the area of social service.

A meeting of minds in a matter so diffuse as the churches and social welfare is a goal worth seeking. But, like most worthy goals, this one is hard to attain. Material on this subject has been presented before. As early as 1914 a *Year Book on the Church and Social Service* was prepared by Harry F. Ward. In 1930 F. Ernest Johnson edited *The Social Work of the Churches*. Successive issues of the *Social Work Yearbook* have carried an article on Protestant social work. But denominational statements comparable in orientation and treatment, have not hitherto been available.

If the foregoing chapters have provided the means toward an improved understanding of important but unsung areas of Christian service, they represent only a first step. As their authors would be quick to admit, these are only summaries of what might profitably have been said. Any comments or generalizations at this point must serve not as a conclusion but as an opening of Christian social welfare to wider discussion. Besides, ecumenical partnership seeks to cultivate fruitful conversation among the churches. Such conversation must be based on facts which afford a two-fold opportunity: first, a comparative study of the basis and development of social welfare in the several denominations; and, second, a penetration of the theology which is fundamental to Christian concern for people in particular need and for the well-being of society as a whole.

After a brief characterization of the denominational statements along lines set forth in the *Guide* (Chapter 1), this chapter follows a more limited sequence in sketching interdenominational developments that bear on the churches and social welfare.

Within the context of faith and life, these statements begin with the subject of authority. Their *basis* of social concern is broadly biblical, with special regard for certain precepts, and above all a recognition of Jesus Christ as authority. As to *motivation*, they reveal an admitted diversity, including the teaching and example of Jesus, God's redemptive love in Christ, missionary and evangelistic intent, the example of other Christians, humanitarian impulses, regard for man's worth and dignity, a passion for justice, and other factors.

In their description of function these statements are fuller. *Social service* in the several communions follows practices which are similar but which arise from a variety of circumstances and are attended by no uniformity of policy. Some, like the Congregational Christian Churches, have initiated services which were later turned over to the community. Others continue to be involved in child and family welfare, health services, chaplaincies, youth and group work, care of the aging, and other services. Larger bodies, like the Episcopal and Lutheran, have engaged extensively in such church-related services. Smaller bodies, like the Friends, have gained distinction in pioneering on other fronts.

In *social action* these communions have varying records. Baptists, Methodists, and Presbyterians, for example, were among the earliest forces for law and moral living on the raw frontier. Among them social reform—later social action—came naturally. Among others it appeared as a more recent development. In recent times, problems with which the churches sought to wrestle included alcoholism, divorce, housing, labor-relations, segregation, refugees, overseas relief, world order, and other issues. Differences of method in social action are apparent, ranging from preaching to legislation, and from community projects to nationwide efforts.

Social education has found its way into the study programs of most of the communions. Variations in emphasis, content, and method are considerable, reflecting the aims and outlooks of the respective churches. *Social research* displays still greater variations. Some, like the Congregational Christians, have been in the forefront of this essential enterprise, and have shared the benefits of their methods with others.

In the realm of comity, *co-operation* has come more readily from some communions than others, depending on circumstances, on theology or on other factors. But in every responding communion the record of co-operation has grown during the past decades. This is reflected in their partnership with others in councils of churches at the local, state, and national levels.

Co-operation with *nonsectarian agencies,* voluntary and public, has likewise engaged these communions. This activity has involved them in the problem of relations between church and state, and of church and community. In general the denominational statements show that participation in the field of social welfare is part of the churches' responsibility for maintaining a viable ethic in a free society. This subject, though treated briefly, is crucial to the role of the churches in providing leadership in the realm of social welfare.

These statements, being primarily descriptive, are only incidentally self-critical. Growing out of a context of history and theology wider than the respective communions, they require at least a short account of historical and theological developments which have affected them all during the present century. What may thus serve as a conclusion to this volume may likewise project the issue of the churches and social welfare on to the stage of more extensive discussion. Therefore the paragraphs below, dealing with the basis, motivation, and practice of Christian welfare work, endeavor to place the denominational statements in the context of modern developments in Christian thought and social change.

The Basis of Christian Welfare Work

Those who formed the Federal Council of Churches in 1908 regarded their action as demonstrative of "the essential oneness of the Christian churches in America in Jesus Christ as their Divine Lord and Savior." Within that oneness, as stated in the constitution, they sought "to promote the spirit of fellowship, service and co-operation." At the same time, the report on The Church and Modern Industry, containing what was later called the "Social Creed" of the churches, affirmed that Jesus Christ "is final authority in the social as in the individual life."

From the beginning, the Council endeavored to preserve a twofold emphasis on the personal and social aspects of the Christian faith. Prevented constitutionally from formulating either a credal statement or a form of worship, it necessarily left the deeper issues of theology to the member churches, while contenting itself with irenic affirmations of faith. These, worded in traditional language, nevertheless breathed the fervor of current concerns.

Prominent among such concerns was the enthusiastic espousal of the social gospel. Although the Council's interest in evangelism continued the personal note, the social note became the more conspicuous. Yet some churches, notably the Lutheran, rejected the social gospel, believing that its link with legislation betrayed the nature of the Evangel. They continued to build up their own agencies. Most churches, however, looked upon the Council as the custodian of the social gospel, adopting its "Social Creed" as a catechism of faith in action, and sought to apply Christian principles to specific situations.

In the trough of economic depression, the Council in 1932 formulated its familiar social platform in expanded form. As the "Social Ideals of the Churches" this new statement spelled out the nature of Christian responsibility and indicated the major areas of concern. "In our extremity," concluded this document, "we therefore turn anew to Christ; for the faith of a great endeavor, for an overwhelming disclosure of God in the life of humanity, for the dedication of innumerable individuals to the creation of a more Christian social order, and for the assurance that what needs to be done with God's help can be done."

The optimism of the churches, once virtually unqualified, became chastened by developments in other parts of the world as well as in America.

In the mid-1930's the once dominant liberalism began to give way to a rising biblical theology, sometimes called neo-protestantism. "The crucial difference," observed John C. Bennett, "between liberalism and neo-protestantism is not to be seen at the level of specific measures of social ethics, but at the deeper level of the theological premises, sanctions and ends which underlie Christian policy in public and private affairs." In short, a return to theology was under way.

This return was evident in the Council's 1936 report on The State of the Church, which asserted: "The great central group in the Church's membership has tended to avoid theology as a subject under taboo. . . . Though we have thus proclaimed a moratorium on theology—pay day has at last arrived. New movements such as communism and fascism are abroad in the world which pretend to furnish men with a complete philosophy of life. Christianity considers these movements to be hostile to its very nature. Christianity knows that it is in for a tremendous struggle with them. But it can never meet them adequately with mere programs for new activities or with appeals to the feelings. It must meet thought with thought, philosophy with philosophy, the new gospels with the Gospel. It must meet the deification of race and class with the message of the incarnation of the most high God in the universal Man who gathers all races and classes into the one body of a common Lord."

Admitting that the churches had made concessions to the world, the report declared: "Our immediate task is to summon our churches to repentance for personal and corporate sin." Such repentance was to lead to a united faith, and to a common conscience for putting this faith into action. The churches would have to be ready to lose in numbers, yet they would then know better on whom to count.

In their respective ways both liberalism and neo-protestantism were Christo-centric. The former appropriated the Jesus of history as Teacher Master, Example for a Godward striving humanity. The latter sought to recover Christ as Savior from the reality of Satan and of an all-corrupting sin, through whom forgiveness is the heart of the Good News and the basis of an ethic acknowledging his Lordship over all life.

It has been said that the first question of the biblical theology is: What does God's sovereignty require of me in this present? The answer was not to be found in a moralizing application of the Sermon on the Mount, but in a new attentiveness to the Word of God. Here the reality of the wrath and judgment of God over the sin of man were again taken seriously. In the atoning death of the Son of God, forgiveness and the gift of new life were vouchsafed the penitent sinner through faith in Christ; while the faith itself was nourished and sustained by the Word, the sacraments, the Church and the Holy Spirit.

This was no straight return to an earlier orthodoxy, but rather a fresh confidence in God amid a human situation which had exploded

114

the optimistic notion of progress. Over against the power and sinister ways of this world, the power of the Gospel is the great "Nevertheless." In obedience to God's authoritative Word, framed in his law, proclaimed by his prophets, and incarnate in his Son, this Christian faith also dares to affirm that social structures and economic conditions can be and should be modified and changed.

An affirmation like this differs from earlier beliefs that social problems can be solved by human effort alone. With fuller insight into the nature of man and the complexities of society, it sees man as a living being whose needs are served not so much by "solutions" as by justice and the attainment of right relations with his fellow men. The kingdom of God is understood not as the attainable and ideal social order, but as God's reign despite man's sin and as God's power over all things. This is regarded not as defeatism but as a turning away from an optimistic teleology and faith in progress to a realistic eschatology and confidence in God. Far from relaxing ethical demands, this places the Christian in new and fruitful tension. This recovery of the biblical message is thus seen to have far-reaching effect on Christian social ethics.

Theological thought in Europe and America and in the younger churches in Asia and Africa has given increasing recognition to the Christo-centric character of biblical authority. Today's ecumenical theology in-the-making is partly indebted to the social gospel. For the way to fuller partnership among the churches was opened by a common concern for people in need. Herein may lie the abiding social sensitivity of a biblically disciplined theology.

It follows that the necessity of anchoring the welfare responsibilities of the churches in the Word of God is gaining ever wider recognition. Biblical authority, when properly understood, communicates itself not through the legalism of proof texts but through a Spirit-filled comprehension of the living Word. This recognition acknowledges the twin elements of freedom and responsibility. On the one hand, it safeguards Christian ethics from being tied to any social or political system and seeks to make ethics an expression of the will of God for man. On the other hand, it exists in a state of tension toward the social environment, knowing that the church cannot leave to others the care and correction of the radical and ever changing needs of men.

The Motivation for Christian Welfare Work

A common Christian faith needs to be activated by a common and informed Christian conscience. Too many Christians, who are getting on in this world tolerably well, seemingly have a strong faith. Yet especially in America such faith may give the impression of being too little touched by the world's great need. It is the informed conscience, then, that must call Christians to action. A recent statement on American abundance and world need caught this meaning in a one-sentence parable: "Bread for myself is a material concern; bread for my brother is a spiritual concern."

Even the Christian who seeks to help others must know that his motives are mixed. His motivations will be determined in some measure by his thoughts, attitudes, and feelings about man, society, and God. As to man, there are at least four views which either overlap or compete. There is, first, the *material* view, regarding man as essentially a physical being whose problems solve themselves as and when his material needs are met. Then there is the *biological* view, conceiving of man as a natural being who requires physical and mental health plus a minimum of obstacles in the way of his natural growth. A third is the *moral* or humanitarian view, understanding man as fundamentally a religious being whose needs are met by having a true scale of values and a clear concept of ultimate purpose. Finally, the *biblical* view of man—at some points overlapping, at others competing with the three previous views—sees him as a total person of different dimensions, rooted in a living relationship with God which involves decision, commitment, and harmonious life in community with fellow men.

With regard to society, the present day extremes place totalitarianism at one pole and individualism at the other. Somewhere in between is the democratic way. It, too, may be lived and explained exclusively on the horizontal level. If so, then human existence is curved in upon itself, is this-worldly, and becomes organized as if God does not exist. Then democracy, like other concepts of society, necessarily avoids the problem of evil and may easily take on the character of religion. As a leader in social work once remarked, "What we used to call God we now call man."

Motivation under these terms springs from faith in man, not from faith in God. It is powered by fellow-feeling, not by divine love. Its service may shine, but ultimately does not warm. An ecumenical conference held near Geneva in 1952 summed up the foregoing views with this word of caution: "The danger even the Christian social worker runs may be to forget the sinful nature of man and the redemptive power of God and to accept a purely humanitarian view of man."

Biblical theology provides a deeper motivation for service because it includes the problem of evil within its scope. When God was in Christ, reconciling the world to himself, the love with which he first loved man was sealed with the dying and risen life of the Son of God. Around this victorious and ever-living Christ a new community, the church, came into being. Called by the Holy Spirit, those who responded also repented. As forgiven sinners, brought into right relationship with God by faith in Christ, they were now in a fellowship which existed not for its own sake but for the sake

116

of the whole world. The fact of their justification by faith, understood as an unmerited gift of God's love, released them from the perpetual motion of self-concern and made them ready for the practice of concern for others. So it is that the Gospel, seen in relation to the function of the Law, awakens a gratitude in the believer that is returned to God in worship and also in service among his needy children. The clue to this return lies in the future.

That Christ has done everything for man's salvation is the great historical fact of the Christian faith. For the believer this fact, while rooted in the past, is illuminated from the future, giving new point to the present. In declaring his coming again in glory to judge all man, Jesus reminds his followers that, in the meantime, he identifies himself with all sorts and conditions of men—the hungry, the thirsty, the naked, the sick, the imprisoned, the strangers. This divine identification with "even the least of these my brethren,"—church membership is here not the question— never allows faith to sink into premature passivity, but prods it to continuing activity.

The facts of the Christian faith are established and sure, but the response, the functional and effective witness to these facts, is to be made in each generation of believers and by every individual among them. Here the motivation of the Christian is joined to responsible action, linking faith and love in hope, and justice and mercy in service.

Social Welfare

In the realm of function terms are subject to change. This is particularly true of the term social service, which gained wide currency earlier in this century. It denoted two types of service. The one was remedial and associated with philanthropy and Christian charity, while the other was preventive and associated with humanitarian reform or action. Today remedial service is included in the term social work, and preventive service is called social action. Both types of service are recognized as interrelated and mutually dependent in the broad field of social service, now frequently called social welfare. With welfare today an admittedly public as well as voluntary responsibility toward society as a whole, the term social welfare denotes not only assistance but also security and justice. It therefore consists in services, action, education, research, planning, and comprehensive patterns of organization and co-operation. The federated efforts among the churches during this century must therefore be seen against this general background.

A common enthusiasm for social service gave the Federal Council of Churches cohesiveness during its formative years. The Council's first specialized unit (1908) was its Commission on Social Service. Out of this commission, or in relation to its interests, other services emerged, including that of research. War-born emergencies made heavy demands. Yet these brought new national, international, and ecumenical perspectives to many forms of service.

Through organizational modifications the interests of the initial Commission on Social Service continue today not only in the National Council's Department of Social Welfare, but also in other departments of its Division of Christian Life and Work, and in such vital units as Research and Survey, United Church Women, and Church World Service. The Division of Home Missions likewise has responsibilities which relate it closely to social welfare.

While common agencies of the churches have thus been alert, dramatic changes have altered the character of social welfare in the extent of its services and in the ideas controlling them. Here it must suffice to make only the briefest reference to the new profession of social work and to the vast body of social data that has arisen in this century. All this has been directed toward helping people to help themselves amid the problems and perplexities of modern living. Since the national bill for welfare services in 1954 totaled $11 billion, and by 1960 is expected to reach $20 billion, social welfare in manifold form is big business and has become an essential element in a democratic society.

The controlling ideas in social welfare are more subtle than dollars, and thus more difficult to appraise. Yet these ideas have a Christian and church-related derivation. It is even possible to describe these ideas as a truncated theology, for in themselves they are incomplete. During the present century these ideas—about man, society, government, and the like—have become increasingly estranged from the Christian origins of this civilization. With due regard for the signs that these origins are once again being recognized and used, the guiding ideas of social welfare today are predominantly humanistic. It is therefore necessary to see the disparity between this secular understanding of the basis and motivation of social welfare, and a Christian understanding as described earlier.

The contrast between non-Christian and Christian modes of understanding may be blamed on that elusive secular malady, "secularism." Yet secularism in welfare work may also be evidence that the churches have relaxed their hold on a continuing responsibility and have failed to grow into the actualities of modern society. The Federal Council's Commission on Social Service early fostered relationships with theological seminaries, schools of social work, and with other institutions, in order to help provide men and women in social service with a "distinctively spiritual point of view." The commission took up relations with the National Conference of Social Work and other organizations, and thus hoped to have a hand in guiding the course of social welfare in this country.

118

That this course would tend toward the development of more effective community responsibility could be understood by most churches as being in keeping with the Elizabethan Poor Law (1601). This law, making little distinction at first between the religious and political aspects of the local unit, the parish, exerted an influence in America from colonial times onward, and continued influential in the thought and practice of welfare until the 1930's. Then, with the large scale entry of government into the field of social welfare the voluntary agencies were suddenly dwarfed. They had to shift from an older and more extensive community-wide concern to the more intensive forms of service that utilized the already present skills of social casework and group work. With government in welfare, whether in relief or social security, the nature of "secularization" here consisted more in a movement of responsibility from private into public hands, than in a premeditated severing of social welfare from theological moorings. The latter had taken place earlier. The American churches had often helped to initiate educational as well as philanthropic services which benefited the community. In return they were ready to accept improved modes of assistance to the needy as devised under auspices other than their own.

Yet the movement which had led the care of human need from the byways of "charity" and relief to the highway of self-respect and social security induced the churches to re-examine their position. How were they related to a situation whose rapid changes had dropped them from a position of leadership to somewhere behind the lines?

In 1948 the Federal Council's Department of Christian Social Relations answered in these words: "The entire field of social work . . . has become highly specialized today. It is only necessary to glance at a program of the National Conference of Social Work for one to realize the truth of this statement. . . . Into this picture steps the Department of Christian Social Relations and attempts to make articulate the concern of the Christian churches for the well-being of the least individual in the community. The traditional Protestant pattern has been to initiate projects, see them launched successfully, and then to withdraw. Coupled with this policy has been a willingness to co-operate with and to use existing secular agencies which are rendering a high standard of service to their clients. Within the past decades there has been a growing concern on the part of many churchmen, clergy, and laity alike, that the increasing secularization of the welfare services and the high intensity of specialization has just about left religion out. Therefore there are denominational leaders, within our own constituency and without, who feel that the time may have arrived when the church, which was the originator of most modern social work, must reassert itself, and reclaim some of the ground it has lost."

With the formation of the National Council of Churches in 1950, this conviction gained momentum. The new Department of Social Welfare was regarded as "a corporate venture undertaken *by* the churches *for* the churches." Yet there was also the recognized weakness that the churches' "method of attack upon social problems and their answer to social needs frequently has been to proceed from the top down." Besides, as stated in the *Biennial Report, 1954:* "There is a great gulf between this department and the mass of church members, many of whom do not dimly suspect the positions to which the department is generally committed. To bridge this gulf requires further strengthening and extension of partnership with the communions and local councils, so that through their offices of social welfare there may be a constant two-way communication between this department and the local churches and church agencies of the communions which it seeks to serve."

In actual accomplishment, the department sponsors the Church Conference of Social Work, publishes the periodical, *Christian Social Welfare,* co-operates with denominational, nonsectarian, and governmental organizations in consultative and other ways. Thus it serves as an instrument of interdenominational and interregional cross-fertilization. "Fresh, illuminating insights into the welfare needs of this generation, novel experiments in meeting needs, convictions forged by success and by failure are brought out of denominational or geographic seclusion for the benefit of the whole church in America."

An impelling necessity therefore gives meaning to the action of the National Council's General Board when, in January 1954, the call went out for a National Conference on the Churches and Social Welfare. This conference, held November 1-4, 1955, in Cleveland, would be the first such undertaking of its kind. Convened by the Department of Social Welfare and the Division of Home Missions, its purpose would be to give delegates from the Council's member denominations, and from state and local councils of churches an opportunity to consider the role and function of the churches in relation to rapidly changing needs in social welfare."

The nature and scope of church-related welfare work, set forth in a companion volume, provides a sweeping view of the profusion of services and activities maintained by the denominations and by councils of churches. These units, by virtue of their relation to the church, are partners meant to enter together into fruitful conversation for the sake of the millions they would seek to serve. Drawn together by the love of God in Jesus Christ, and sent forth in his name, they render the one kind of welfare that has a future.